RABINDRANATH TAGORE

SONAR TAREE
(Golden Craft)

TRANSLATION BY BROTHER JAMES

The University Press Limited

The University Press Limited
Red Crescent House
61 Motijheel C/A
P. O. Box 2611
Dhaka 1000
Bangladesh
Fax : (88 02) 9565443
E-mail: upl@bangla.net
Website: www.uplbooks.com

First published 1986
Second impression 2008

Translation Copyright © Brother James

All rights are reserved. No part of this publication may be reproduced or transmitted in any form or by any means without prior permission in writing from the publisher. Any person who does any unauthorised act in relation to this publication may be liable to criminal prosecution and civil claims for damages.

Cover design by *Lala Rukh Selim (Toree)*

ISBN 984 05 1071 1

Published by The University Press Limited, Dhaka and book design by Ashim K. Biswas. Produced by AMS Enterprise and printed at the Akota Offset Press, 119 Fakirapool, Dhaka, Bangladesh.

FOREWORD (XV-XVI)

ACKNOWLEDGEMENT (XVII)

NOTES: SONAR TAREE (1891–1893)

GOLDEN CRAFT (1-2)

- The poet says he is the boatman. He does not know where he got these things or where he is taking them. The Golden Craft takes the fruit of his labour, but leaves him behind, This piece and its interpretation are among the most controversial in Bengali literature.
- Sraban—second month of the rainy season: mid-July to mid-August

BIMBABOTI (2-5)

- a children's story
- sari—a long, wide length of cloth draped round the body; worn by girls and women
- mantra—mystical/magic formula to achieve a goal
- modesty scarf—a piece of cloth worn by women to cover the breast

Moral: one dies in the flames of one's jealousy

A CHILDHOOD EVENING (6-7)

- anchal—end of a sari
- betel-nut—areca nut: sliced thin, it is chewed with pan leaf, lime, spices

THE PRINCE AND THE PRINCESS (8-9)

- a folktale

SLEEPING (9-12)

- Sleeping Beauty—a folktale
- anchal—end of a sari
- lampblack—soot used as ink

AWAKED (12-15)
- based on a folktale
- kadamba—a flowering tree
- anchal—end of a sari
- shefalika/shefali—weeping nycthantes—a tree that blossoms at night and sheds white blossoms
- professional singer—one who sang the praises of the king

YOU AND WE (15-17)
- youth and adults: the young and the old
- anchal—end of a sari
- mantra—magic formula

GOLDEN BANGLES (17-18)
- praise of the devoted mother and wife
- bonds, bands, bangles

SPENDING THE RAINY SEASON (18-22)
- Indra—Hindu deity presiding over the atmosphere
- Indra's horse's neighing—thunder
- Ashar—mid-June to mid-July, first month of the rainy season
- Meghdut—Cloud Messenger, a poem epic by Kalidas
- desh & mollar modes, tunes (Indian music)
- Radha/Radhika—ladylove of Krishna
- Sraban—second month of the rainy season: mid-July to mid-August
- Brindaban—where Krishna frolicked with Radha and the milkmaids

HING TING CHHAT (22-29)
- title: gibberish. resembling Sanskrit sounds
- mocks those who pay attention to dreams and useless events and miss the grandeur of living

- abatangsha—learned men who add glory to the family
- tuft—tiki—uncut tuft of hair to maintain personal holiness
- Vedas—the four sacred books of the Hindus
- Mlechchha—non-Aryan tribe of ancient India; non-Hindu
- Shiva—one of the 3 gods in the Hindu triad; representing the principle of destruction and also the reproductive/restoring power

TOUCHSTONE (29-32)
- Some search for the unattainable to make life easy. Meanwhile they lose life's simple gifts and joys
- touchstone—philosopher's/alchemist's stone: a stone or substance that would change base metals into gold; a black stone to test the purity of gold and silver
- testing streak—notion from Hindu mythology
- Lakshmi—Hindu goddess of wealth and prosperity
- guru—an ascetic; a spiritual teacher
- goddess of the western sky: one of the goddesses presiding over the 10 directions

A VAISNAB POEM (33-35)
- a Vaisnab. n.—a worshipper of Vishnu; a follower of Chaitanya, a 16th century Bengali who was a passionate devotee of the love of Krishna and Radha; for him the highest bliss was to identify himself with Radha and so submit himself to the passionate embraces of his Lord: the soul must play the woman in its dealing with God, the universal male (zaehner); this cult has influenced many subcontinent cults
- Brindaban—scene of frolicking by Krishna and Radha and the milkmaids
- Sraban—second month of the rainy season: mid-July to mid-August

- kadamba—a flowering tree
- Radha/Radhika—Krishna's ladylove (in his 1902 Noibedya Tagore rejects such emotionalism.)

TWO BIRDS (36-37)
- as a boy Tagore was closely confined and felt like a caged bird; freedom or enslavement with security?
- Tagore shows up those who love their bonds

MOON IN THE SKY (37-40)
- striving for the impossible while disdaining the good things of life ends in futility
- anchal—end of a sari
- ghat—a sloping landing place for boats; a brick-built stairway for bathing or for getting water
- purabee—a soft, evening song mode

BREAK IN THE SONG (40-44)
- conflict between the old and the new; art has to be appreciated
- Indian musical modes/tunes: kafi, agaman, bijoya, bhoopali, multani, shahana, imankallan
- Holi—festival commemorating the throwing of red powder at one another by Krishna and the milkmaids who loved him and frolicked with him and Radha
- Gokul—a village inn. India where krishna and his brother were raised, formerly inhabited by milkmen
- tambura/tanpura—a stringed musical instrument that helps a singer keep perfect tune
- betel-nut—sliced nut & pan leaf & lime
- guru—the king, his master

I WON'T LET YOU GO (44-50)
- parting is painful; death, progress, development, duty, growth etc. pay no heed to attachments or links

- Aswin/Ashin—second month of the autumn: mid-September to mid-October; rains are over, flood waters recede, new growth
- puja vacation—long October vacation for a string of Hindu worship festivals
- sari—a length of cloth draped round the body, worn by women and girls

TO THE OCEAN (51-55)
- Bay of Bengal viewed from Puri, Orissa state
- Vedas—4 Hindu religious books
- vedic mantras/hymns/incantations
- Indra—Hindu god, king of the gods and goddesses, god of the atmosphere

AWAITING (55-60)
- In 1868, when he was seven, his elder brother Jyoti married Kadambaree, practically Robi's age. When he was 14, his mother died and Jyoti took him in. The young wife "smothered this gifted brother-in-law with affection". She loved poetry and with Jyoti, encouraged Robi. Kadambaree died in 1884, the second very dear one snatched away by death. In his old age Tagore wrote: "When the first daughter-in-law came to our home, my mind was like a boat at anchor, but the tide came roaring in to toss it about. Providence brought me bounty overflowing the measured ration of happiness…"
- bairab—a solemn musical mode
- life-bird—jiban debata— "the presiding deity of the poet's life, the poet himself, the Inner Self; not God" (Thirty years later Tagore could not say what he had in mind)
- let death come when he has enjoyed life more fully
- matted hair of Shiva

CREATIONS OF MY MIND (60-72)
- poetry, beauty personified, his beloved
- beena—double guitar with 7 strings, yielding a jingling sound
- anchal—end of a sari
- Padma—his rowed and poled houseboat
- shefali—weeping nycthantes, a tree that blossoms at night with copious white flowers
- shahana, multan—Indian musical modes
- bakal—a flowering tree
- Sraban—second month of the rainy season: mid-July to mid-August
- previous existence/path of rebirth: Tagore was a Brahmo, but he used the imagery of his culture

NOT APPRECIATED (72-74)
- one's work, one's ideas are not always appreciated—a love sonnet

BY RIVER (75-76)
- the poet remembers his wife at home
- travelling by houseboat, shelter is sought in a canal

TEMPLE (76-79)
- after viewing the temple of Jaganath/Lord of the universe/Vishnu or Krishna, his 8th avatar (at Puri, Orissa)
- the poet had shut out the world to worship his deity; then the thunderous voice of humanity breaks in and smashes his shrine to pieces; the deity smiles because the poet is in union with his fellowmen
- mantra—mystic hymn or verse
- deity—a god or goddess—an image in wood, stone, etc. to represent a being regarded or worshipped as having power over nature and control over human affairs

UNIVERSAL DANCE (80-83)
- the Great Musician plays His music in the spheres, in cosmic forces, in the eternal dance of life and death and calls on all to shed their bonds and bondages. In the heart "Someone is playing day and night." The poet wants a united mankind to move forward.

HARD TO KNOW (83-85)
- a love sonnet, a man-woman encounter

SWINGING (85-88)
- the titanic struggle between the 'self' and the soul—between pran (soul), the beloved and 'I' the lover. The 'self' has rocked the soul into a stupor with love and tenderness. The tempest comes and the soul is roused from death like sleep. The soul is his beloved, his friend the poet himself. Tagore wants the truth to replace the dream, (In many other poems Tagore wants the storm to come and rouse him)

HEART-JAMUNA (89-90)
- a love sonnet, an offering of his love
- the poet uses the Jamuna rather than the Ganges because the Jamuna is the river of love: Radha and Krishna romped about there; the Tajmahal, a monument to love, is there
- anchal—a tree with colourful blossoms

PASSING YOUTH (90-91)
- a love sonnet; lost youth is regretted
- Jamuna, the river of love, in India

FULL AUGUST (92-93)
- the month of Badra, mid-August to mid-September; the rivers are full and overflowing; it is late autumn, the end of the rainy season

- bakul—a flowering tree
- the paddy/rice fields are full
- doyel—black and white magpie-robin

REPROACH (93-95)
- a love sonnet

SHYNESS (95-97)
- a love sonnet
- anchal—the end of a sari

PRIZE (97-117)
- a poet just wants his art, his work appreciated
- Saraswati—Hindu goddess of speech and learning
- Lakshmi—Hindu goddess of wealth, prosperity, luck, beauty and grace
- Bharati—Saraswati, goddess of speech
- anchal—end of a sari
- nawab—a feudal prince
- brahminee—wife of a brahmin
- brahmin—member of the highest/priestly caste: an officiating Hindu pirest
- Vaisnab (a)—a worshipper of the god Vishnu
- daughter's needs—wedding dowry etc.
- Lake Manashi—a big lake in the Himalayas
- beena—7-stringed double guitar
- Ram—an incarnation of Vishnu; the hero of the Ramayana
- Sita—wife of Ram
- kshatriya—member of the warrior caste
- Bharat—India
- Holi—Hindu festival commemorating the throwing of red powder at one another by Krishna and the milkmaids enamoured of him
- Mother Bharati—goddess of speech
- palanquin—covered litter for one person, carried on poles by two or more men

- Lakshmi, the goddess of wealth, got the poet recognition from the king and from his wife
- Saraswati/Bharati won a prize for the poet; the two goddesses are united in the bond of the garland prize

MOTHER EARTH (117-127)
- anchal—the end of a sari
- Mother Earth is Tagore's Mother; he wants to be united with nature, with the whole world and partake of its joys; he wants every place to be his home: he wants to live like all the peoples of the earth
- celestial green wishing-cow: mythological, grants wishes

ILLUSIONISM (127-128)
- a sonnet against those Hindus who think that the material world is an illusion

A GAME (128-129)
- a sonnet—Tagore enjoys God's picturesque world; play the game of life; He often alludes to God's action in the world as His khela, sport, game

A BOND (129)
- a sonnet—yes, we are bound to earth and to each other, but with them we long for happiness and for "the life that is difficult to attain"

MOTION (130)
- a sonnet—he does not want to tear the bonds with everyone else, he wants to go forward with everyone

SALVATION (130-131)
- a sonnet—salvation/freedom is to be attained in the company of all men

POWERLESS (131-132)
- a sonnet—our Earthen Mother cannot supply all our needs; that's no reason to leave her

POOR ONE (132)
- a sonnet—Earth is deficient but is still "the shadow of heaven"

SELF-DEDICATION (132-133)
- a sonnet—the poet will beautify earth, setting her joy songs and sad songs to music

FIRM REMEMBRANCE (133-134)
- a sonnet—this heavenly earth is real, it is not an illusion

THORN TREE (134-136)
- soft, gentle, joy-giving beauty is mocked and decried by the ugly, the harsh, the tough

AIMLESS JOURNEY (136-138)
- the poet is asking Beauty, his poetry-goddess, where she is taking him in the Golden Craft; the western ocean is shoreless
- the ten direction-maidens—10 goddesses presiding over the 10 directions

FOREWORD

When Tagore was in a very low class, he had this experience: "Suddenly I came to a (Bengali) rhymed sentence, 'It rains, the leaves tremble.' At once I came to a world where I recovered my full meaning. My mind touched the creative realm of expression, and, at that moment, I was no longer a mere student with his mind ruffled by spelling lessons, enclosed by a classroom." A nephew, older by seven years, showed him how to make rhymes. Somendra, an older brother encouraged him.

When he was about twenty years old and living in Calcutta with his elder brother and his wife, this happened: "The glow of the sunset combined with the wan twilight in a way that gave the approaching evening a special wonderful attraction. Even the walls of the adjoining house seemed to grow beautiful. The effect of the evening had been from within me; its shade had obliterated myself. When the self was rampant during the day, everything I perceived was mingled with it and hidden by it. Now that the self was put into the background, I could see the world in its own true aspect. That aspect has nothing of triviality in it, it is full of beauty and joy."

Looking toward the end of the same Sadar Street, he had this experience: "The sun was just rising through the leafy tops of the trees. As I continued to gaze, all of a sudden a covering seemed to fall away from my eyes, and I found the world bathed in a wonderful radiance with waves of beauty and joy swelling on every side. This radiance pierced in a moment through the folds of sadness and despondency which had accumulated over my heart, and flooded it with this universal light." That day he wrote "The Awaking of the Waterfall."

"Sonar Taree was my first popular book, the first that gathered a group of readers who became my admirers. Perhaps Manashi was the first to do this, but Sonar Taree gave me my place.... Most of the Gitanjali pieces were written at Santiniketan (1907–1910) ... I used to write almost every day and sometimes at night. I did not intend to publish them. I knew people would be disappointed, and would say that after Sonar Taree they were poor. But I knew they were very intimately my own." (Rabindranath Tagore got the Nobel prize in literature in 1913.)

ACKNOWLEDGEMENT

Sonar Taree would not have been translated and published without the skill, intelligence and care of Manwara Hussain.

— Brother James

GOLDEN CRAFT

'Clouds are rumbling in the sky,
    It's now the dense monsoon season,
I'm sitting alone on the river bank
    without any expectation.
Countless platforms are heaped with paddy,
    Harvesting is over.
The current of the brimming river
    is as sharp as a razor.
The monsoon came
    even as the paddy was being cut.

Here lies a small field,
    I'm all alone,
The swirling waters
    are playing their winding game.
On the other side of the river
    I see a village limned in dark lines
        in the shade of the trees blackened more
            by gray clouds at dawn.
On this side there is a small field,
    I'm all alone.

Who is it that's coming to the shore,
    singing as he rows—
        it seems to me I know him,
Without looking in any direction
    he speeds a long with full sail,
        The helpless waves are split in two—
        It seems to me I know him.

Dearly beloved, where is it you're going,
    to what distant place—
Just this once
    turn your craft around, come to the shore.

Then go wherever you please,
    Dispose of it according to your pleasure—
Just smile awhile, come to the shore
    and take away my golden paddy.

Take on to your craft as much as you wish;
    Is there more ? Nothing is left,
        I've loaded the craft with my all.
Whatever I've heedlessly brought to the shore
    all these days
        I've loaded it all layer upon layer—
        Now kindly take me too.

There's no space, no space—
    The craft is small
        and filled with my golden paddy.
Dense clouds are rambling
    throughout the Sraban sky,
I've been left behind
    on the lonely bank of the river—
All that I had
    was taken by the golden craft.

BIMBABOTI
A LEGEND

With great care the queen adorns herself,
    braids her hair,
        skillfully puts on her blue sari
            soft and cooling like a new cloud
Slowly she removes the secret cover
    and brings out the magic mirror.
After reciting a mantra, she asks the mirror,
    "Who is the most beautiful woman
        in the world ?"
Slowly there appears in the mirror a face

exceedingly charming and pleasant.
On seeing the face
    her heart is torn in shock—
        it is the princess Bimbaboti, her step-
                daughter;
            She is the most beautiful woman
            in the world.

The next day the queen put on a coral necklace,
    Loosening her hairdo,
        she let her hair fall to her knees,
She pulled over her breast the edge of her sari,
    the tint of a blush.
Setting the golden mirror on her lap
    and reciting a mantra she asked:
        "Tell me truly.
            Who is the most beautiful woman
                in the world ?"
In the mirror there again appeared
    that moon-like face.

Trembling and smarting with rage, the queen said:
    "I garlanded her with poisonous flowers,
        yet she didn't die an agonizing death,
            that step-daughter of mine !
                She is the most beautiful woman
                in the world !"

The following day
    the queen bolted the door of her bedroom,
She put on a pearl necklace,
    painted a vermillion dot on her forehead,
        darkened the area around her eyes.
She donned a blood-red skirt
    and a golden modesty scarf.
Addressing the mirror, she said:
    "Tell me the truth.

Who is the most beautiful woman
    in the world ?"
In the shiny, golden mirror
    the same smiling face became visible.
Overcome with jealousy,
    the queen tossed about on her bed.
With loud lamentations she cried out:
    "I had her firmly tied up
        and left in the forest.
    Still she hasn't died,
        that step-daughter of mine !
            She is the most beautiful woman
                in the world !"

The very next day
    the queen adorned herself
        with new ornaments.
Bending forward
    she put up her hair in a new style.
Carefully she wrapped around her hips
    a new skirt glowing like fresh sunlight.
She held the mirror before her
    and, after reciting the magic words, she said,
        "Tell me truly:
            Who is the most beautiful woman
                in the world ?"
That smiling face blossomed out
    in the magic mirror.

The queen flared up into a passion.
    "I tricked her into eating poisonous fruit,
        still she hasn't died,
            that step-daughter of mine !
    She is the most beautiful woman
        in the world !"

Scrupulously, the next day
  the queen adorned herself with gold and gems.
Conceitedly she addressed the mirror;
    "Be truthful !
      Whose is the most beautiful body
        in the world ?"
Two smiling and charming faces
  were reflected in the mirror.
The prince and the princess
  were side by side in wedding apparel.
Utterly mortified
  the queen struck her bosom and screamed,
"Before my eyes I saw her die !
  Through whose love and affection
    was she able to survive,
      that step-daughter of mine ?
        She is the most beautiful woman
          in the world !"

With sand the queen began to rub the golden mirror,
  still the reflection didn't go away.
She smeared it with soot,
  still the picture remained,
She put it in the fire,
  but the gold didn't melt.
With all her might
  she threw it on the ground,
    but it didn't break into pieces.
Suddenly the queen fell to the ground
  and died.
All the diamonds and gems on her limbs
  sparkled like fire.
On the face of the mirror lying at her side
  the two charming faces kept smiling.
Bimbaboti, the step-daughter of the queen,
  was the most beautiful woman
    in the world.

A CHILDHOOD EVENING

Slowly and softly there spreads out
    in all directions weariness and peace
        and the darkness of evening
            that blankets all
                like the anchal of a mother's sari.
Standing alone,
    I'm gazing westward,
I'm getting engrossed in the profound depth,
    I'm gradually filling my life
        with today's picture—
            the desolate river bank, the setting sun,
                the pale, failing light—
            the weeping sun with its weary eyes
                is a doleful sight, stolid, speechless—
            this profound melancholy,
                this fatigue and languor
                    on water, on land in the universe.
All of a sudden a boy on foot bursts into song
        some place, on some village path
            in a dark grove.
His impassioned voice,
        full-throated, carefree, fearless,
            is trembling in a high key.
It seems as if the sharp and high-pitched melody
        will cut the dusk in two.
I cannot see the shore.
    In front of me, at the extreme end of the field,
        there, to the north,
            at the side of the sugarcane field,
                there are plantain and betel-nut trees
                and thick clumps of bamboo.
In the midst of these
        the village is taking a rest,
            My eyes run over the scene.
A cow-herd's son is returning home, singing,

He's not thinking of anything,
> He's not gazing at the heavens,
> > He has no past, he has no future.
As I hear and see all this I recall
> that evening in my childhood.
How much gossip, how many childish games,
> we three: friends lying on the bed—
This is not a tale about today,
> So many days have passed away !
Hasn't the world grown old yet ?
> Hasn't it forgotten how to play ?
> > Doesn't drowsiness overcome the eyes,
> > calm and cooling ?
Didn't it exchange firm enlightenment
> for the toys of childhood ?
In the still twilight as I stand here
> in the empty field
> > listening to someone's song, I recall
> > the fresh smiling faces,
> > > the fresh happiness of full young hearts,
> > > the improbable remarks, the novel fantasies,
> > > the groundless trust,
> > > > unlimited aspirations, endless faith,
on countless river banks, in many mango groves,
> at the side of temples resounding
> > with the clanging of bells,
> at the side of many paddy fields,
> > on the banks of many pools,
> > in home after home.
Standing in the dark I see
> in the light of the stars,
> > in the limitless universe,
> > the earth filled with boys and girls,
> > > with evening beds, the faces of mothers,
> > > with the light of lamps.

THE PRINCE AND THE PRINCESS
A FAIRY TALE

—in the morning—

The prince used to go to the primary school,
    The princess went there too.
They used to meet on the path,
    No one knows when this happened.
The princess stayed some distance away,
    Flowers from her hair fell off at times
The prince used to pick these up
    together with flowers of wild creepers.
The prince used to go to the primary school,
    The princess went there too.
Flowers bloomed on both sides of the path,
    Birds sang in the trees.
The princess walked in front,
    The prince walked in back.

—at noon—

The princess sat on a higher floor, reading,
    The prince sat on a lower floor.
Opening his books, he studied some languages,
    He did his sums and drew some figures.
The princess could not remember her lessons,
    The book fell out of her hands,
The prince came and picked it up for her,
    then he went back to his sums.
The princess sat above, reading,
    The prince sat below.
At noon the heat was intense,
    A cuckoo was cooing.
The prince stared upward,
    The princess stared downward.

—in the evening—

The prince went back to his room,
    The princess returned to hers,
Removing her pearl necklace,
    she played with it.

On the path it fell off,
    The prince picked it up,
In a fit of forgetfulness
    he gave the girl his necklace of gems.
The prince returned to his room,
    The princess went back to hers.
The tired sun set at last
    on the far end of the river bank.
Both of them finished their lessons,
    They went to their own places.
        —at night—
The princess was lying on a golden cot,
    She dreamt of charming things.
The prince was lying on a silver cot,
    he saw salmon's joy-lit face.
Joys and sorrows came and went,
    At times her heart beat violently,
Sometimes a smile trembled on her lips,
    Then again her, eyes filled with tears.
The king's daughter saw someone's face,
    The prince saw someone's smile.
The rain fell in incessant streams,
    The clouds rumbled, the wind blew madly.
Her head was on the pillow, her dress was rumpled,
    The night was spent in dreams.

SLEEPING

I, a prince, was roaming far and wide,
    beyond the corners of the world.
I saw all the beautiful faces,
    There was none left to see.
One talked with me a bit,
    Another looked at me but lowered her gaze;
Another ones smile cut like a knife,
    Another's smile was like tears to her.

Some proudly went back home,
    Some looked back again and again, weeping;
Some said not a word to others,
    Others slowly sang songs.
This way I wandered all over the world;
    Far away, beyond an extensive wilderness
a princess was sleeping in a sleeping land,
    I placed a garland round her neck.

One night, during my fresh youth,
    I woke up startled from a dream;
        I come out and looked around at the world.
In the eastern sky Venus was barely visible,
    The night was turning to dawn;
Awaking was blossoming out in a corner of the sky,
    On earth all was in the grip of sound sleep.
In front of me lay a long highway,
    Rows of trees lined both sides.
Staring into the distance,
    I thought to myself—
'Today, at the close of this night,
    there is, in some new place in this world,
        a princess, sleeping and dreaming,
            brightening her bed
                as white and soft as the froth of milk.'

Then I went out riding on my horse,
    I had to cross oh so many lands and countries;
On a dull gray evening
    I reached the gate of sleep-land.
There everyone lay motionless and unconscious;
    Not a single creature was awake;
On the river bank, amid the sweet notes of the stream,
    a huge palace was sleeping,
I was afraid to tread there,
    lest, in an instant, the whole land awake.
Carefully I entered the palace,
    my misgivings preceding me,

The king was sleeping, the queen's mother was
                                                sleeping,
   The king's brother was sleeping with the prince.
In one room a gem-studded lamp was burning,
    There a princess was sleeping.
The bed was as spotless as a lotus,
    Her delicately slim and lovely body
        was sunk deep in the soft bed;
Steadfastly I gazed at her face,
    Pain-like bliss filled my heart
Clusters of hair, like clouds,
    spread over the pillow;
One arm was over her breast,
    Another lay extended on one side.
Her anchal was loose on one side,
    Her bodice was becoming untied;
Two flowers of worship, it seemed to me,
    lay covered by a leaf-cup,
I looked long at her,
    What I saw was beyond compare—
        a dream in the land-of-sleep,
            the princess deep in her bed,
                alone in her perfect loveliness and charm.

Tightly I pressed my arms to my excited breast,
    not able to check the trembling of my heart;
Sitting on the floor, I bowed my head
    and kissed her closed eyes.
With rapt attention
    I beheld the pupils of her eyes,
        partly visible behind her eyelids;
Through the partly open door I strove to see
    whatever there was in this secret abode.
On a piece of birch bark I wrote with lamoblack
    my name and address;
I wrote: 'Deep-in-sleep,
    I offer you my heart, my love.'

To the necklace of gems strung with gold thread
 I carefully tied my note.
The princess was sleeping in the land-of-sleep,
 I had put a garland round her neck.

AWAKED

The sleeping land woke up,
 A sweet, murmuring sound could be heard,
The birds woke up on the branches,
 Bees began their humming,
In the stable the horses woke up,
 so did the elephants.
Awaking in the games room,
 the wrestler began to expand his chest again,
The night watchmen woke up on the road
 as did the doorkeeper at the door,
All the men and women woke up
 and looked up at the sky to see what time it was.
The emperor woke up, so did the queen mother;
 Rubbing his eyes, the king's brother got up,
There was the odour of incense in the private room,
 the gem-studded lamp was still burning,
The princess woke up on her bed and asked,
 'Who garlanded me !'

She spread the loosened end of her sari
 over her bosom.
Looking at herself,
 she thrilled in embarrassment.
Bustling confusedly,
 she looked about with startled glances—
She was alone in the room
 and the flame of the lamp was burning evenly.
Taking off her garland,
 she held and read the note

which was carefully embroided with gold thread.
She read the name, she read the address,
she spread the note on her lap and kept reading it.
After lying down, the princess sat up
    and wondered, 'I was sleeping in my room
        in complete solitude;
           Who garlanded me !'

In the newly-awaked arbour the cuckoo cooed,
    In all directions everything was overwhelmed
        by the kiss of spring.
The breeze burst into the room,
    excited and delighted,
        wafting the fragrance of fresh flowers.
The professional singer was up, singing
    the victory song that honoured the king,
A charming tune issued from the flute
    at the palace door.
Having filled her pitcher with water,
    the village girl was going
        by the shade-cool riverside road,
Her ankle-bells were ringing,
    her bangles were jingling,
The leaves were rustling
    as they trembled on the forest path,
With half-closed eyes the princess was wondering
    'Who put the garland on me !'

Once again she put on the garland,
    Again she took it off,
She raised it to her bosom
    and held it tightly,
Spreading it out on her bed,
    she gazed at it with desirous longing,
It was as if by doing so
    she could learn more about the giver.

Oh how many sounds there are in the world,
    sounds for many reasons,
There is a secret word
    that no one talks about,
The wind was whistling near her ear,
    Only the cuckoo cooed without tiring.
In her lonely room
    her heart became real restless,
After lying down,
    she sat up all alone and wondered,
        'Who put the garland on me ?'

How hero-like his appearance !
    How charming his good looks !
What unquenchable desire
    shone in his bright eyes !
She felt that she had seen him
    in her dreams, but had forgotten all,
        There only remained boundless amazement,
It seemed
    he was sitting beside her,
        holding her hand—
  Even now her whole body thrilled at his touch,
Taken by surprise,
    she covered her face with her hands,
        Her peace of mind was shattered—
At that moment
    why didn't the brazen-faced lamp go out !
From her neck she tore off the garland
    as if it were searing lightning,
Throwing herself on the bed,
    the princes wondered,
        'Who put the garland on me !'
Wearily and in such fashion
    went her days and nights,
That spring bade farewell
    with a gift of jasmines,

With endless clouds the rains came
    and poured down in incessant streams—
In the arbour another kind of jasmine bloomed,
    so did the scented-flower kadamba,
Then came autumn with her cloudless smile
    and a full-moon garland,
At night the shefalika showered her white flowers
    and excited the whole arbour.
Next came winter
    with her long, sad nights,
On all sides tears of joy were shed
    by the dew-drenched, multi-petalled jasmines.
Spring came again,
    bearing her basket of flowers,
Sitting alone by the window,
    the princess wondered,
        'Who put the garland on me !'

YOU AND WE

All of you go away with a smile
    just like a flowing, babbling river.
Standing on the bank,
    we're looking at you;
        So many desires are suffering
            from suppressed grief.
You're happily whispering to yourselves,
    The glow of happiness lights up your eyes,
                              your faces,
Your lotus-like feet tread the earth,
    Your golden ankle bells are jingling.

You're tying merry-making to your limbs and bodies,
    Beautiful creepers encircle your arms,
Laughter rings out from your charming gestures,
    Secret messages are flowing from eye to eye.

Your eyes downcast,
  you're stringing flowers together by yourselves,
    With the aid of mirrors,
      you're dressing your hair,

You're playing a game by yourselves
    in the secret of your hearts—
      What are you thinking of?
        How are you passing your days?

In the twinkling of an eye
  your curling tresses fly up in the air,
Bending over slightly, you spread out your anchal—
  In a second and without opening your eyes,
    you shoot a sidelong glance,
      hastily looking for someone.

Your immense youthfulness wants to burst out,
  wants to enjoy itself wholeheartedly,
You're regulating it by the way you dress,
  Still in hundreds of ways,
    it blossoms out beautifully,
      flashing and spilling over as you move about.

We're fools! We don't know how to talk,
  We talk about what we don't want to talk about.
At the wrong time
  we take our hearts and cast them at your feet—
    and keep gaping at you.
You observe this and whisper among yourselves,
    You and your friends are beside yourselves
        with mirth,
You draw the anchal across your bosom
    and go away smiling,
      having got more than you had expected.

We run about in outbursts of passion
    like a mighty, unfeeling storm,

Spreading over the whole sky in the vast darkness,
    we want to break our own hearts.
You, the lightning, are laughing
    as you look at us,
You split the darkness
    and pierce our heart of hearts—
Drawing a line of fire on the surface of the sky,
    in the twinkling of an eye you go away,
        having fooled us.

God created our bodies neglectfully.
    He didn't fit our eyes and ears
        with the means of expressing ourselves.
We don't know any enchanting or pleasing mantras:
    How can we say what's on our minds ?
Where are you ? Where are we !
    At some auspicious time
        won't we get together ?
You'll go away laughing,
    We'll stand still as we are now.

GOLDEN BANGLES

Oh what grace and beauty are yours,
    oh lady of the home !
You are the captive of very pleasant
    love and tenderness in a home
        full of doleful weeping,
            full of poverty and distress !

So, on your arms there are charming bonds,
   two golden bracelets that adorn your whole body
      with the sign of well-being,
         very pleasing to the eyes of all.

The arms of a man are free of bonds
    and calloused by the struggle of life;

They are always free like lightning,
    like flaming arrows,
        in all battles and conflicts,
            in all hard work.

But you are imprisoned
    in the midst of love, affection, kindness—
        only doing all useful work,
            only doing things for others
                and being helpful day and night.

No one knows
    who has drawn on your arms
        two golden encircling lines,
            two golden bracelets.

SPENDING THE RAINY SEASON

Calcutta, the capital;
    a wooden cubicle on one side of the roof
        on the second floor;
Light comes from the east,
    The breeze comes through the south door.

My bedding is spread out on the floor,
    I keep my head near the door
        and let my eyes rove about outside—
Hundreds of mansion roofs are frowning at the sky
    and hiding so many mysteries.
There is a bit of greenery near the window
    in a corner of the parapet,
All day long a young sacred fig tree
    is watching the dancing of her shadow.
Along the whole horizon the monsoon is descending,
    turning everything inky black;

Throughout the whole sky Indra's horse is neighing,
    Lightning is flashing here and there.
At all times, on all sides
    the rain is falling in constant streams,
        stealing from the view of this little end room
        the entire outside world.

Sitting alone, I'm enjoying myself
    reading the story of Meghdut for a few days—
Day and night the wind is greatly frenzied
    With fruitless agitation—
I'm looking back into the past—
    I go over the mountains, rivers, towns
        of cloud-covered India
           during long-ago monsoons—
Oh how many sweet-sounding names,
    how many lands, how many villages I cross
        as my gaze roves.
I know them both quite well,
    the separated ones, the lover and the beloved,
        the world's two people on opposite shores—
There is great attraction between them,
    There is a great distance between them,
        They fancy oh so many things !
In a corner of a room
    Yaksha's wife counted the days with flowers,
        After seeing all this, I come back.
The rain keeps falling with the rumbling of clouds,
    On my lap I carefully place the lyrics of
                           Gobindadas.
Modulating my voice again and again
    as if singing,
        I read about the monsoon tryst of Radha—
There was deep darkness on the bank of the Jamuna,
    Youthful Radha is looking for the arbour hut,
        not heeding the difficulties at night.
Rain keeps pouring down endlessly,
    The forest is at a great distance;

The doors of the houses are all barred,
    No one is with her save the youth Madan.'

The monsoon is coming to an end,
    I compose monsoon tunes
        mingled with desh and mollar modes.
Opening the first page of the Songs of Gitagobinda
    I sing 'The sky is pleasantly soft with clouds.'
At still midnight the rain comes splashing down,
    I'm lying down in blissful wakefulness
        and recollect that very song:
            'The night is deep with Sraban,
                The thick clouds are rumbling.'
With only a loose piece of rag on her body,
    she is lying down and frolicking on a rich bed;
        Immensely happy, she is sunk in sleep—
That very picture comes to mind:
    the secret dream of Radhika in ancient Brindaban.
She is breathing softly,
    There is a smile on her lips,
        Her closed eyelids are quivering;
Her head is on her arm,
    She is sleeping all alone,
        The lamp is giving off a feeble flame.
Clouds are thundering on the mountain peaks,
    The rain is streaming down on the branches,
        All night long the frogs are croaking—
Anything can happen at such a time,
    Surely the companion of her dreams
        will come alone into the room.
What a pity ! When she awakes alone
    at the end of the dream,
        overwhelmed with pleasure,
            she sees that the lamp is about to go out,
                The watchman is shouting out the time.
The rain is pouring down faster,
    The clouds rumble from time to time,

The chirping of crickets pervades the whole earth.
This night, overcast with thick clouds.
    mingled with dreams and wakefulness—
      Oh how my heart is acting up !

I take up some books, I look through them casualty,
    So go my days and nights.
I pick up some foreign poetical works,
    I idly turn the pages—
Where is the shade of the rainy season,
    Where is the illusion of dark clouds,
   Where is the crashing sound of pouring rain,
Where is the profound separation of that life
    that is full of leisure, fully absorbed in itself !
My interior and my exterior fill
    with the same tune as the rain,
      with a torrential downpour of songs.
The shores of my heart are not only filled
    but overflow to a great distance;
      Alas ! Where now are the foreign poems !
Then I throw the books aside
    and spread out a seat by the door
      and sit absent-mindedly—
There's nothing I have to do,
    so I idly gaze outside and wonder
      how I'll pass these long days.
I bend over and carefully compose something
    all day long—
One by one and without stopping,
    I want to write short stories
      after my own heart,
Ordinary people, simple lives, common pains,
    the usual sad events,
      quite plain and easy to understand—
Thousands of these forgotten happenings
    go streaming by day after day—
      (I'll take) a few of their tears.

There will be no descriptive glamour,
    no collections of marvellous happenings,
      no information, no advice.
After finishing each story,
    the reader will feel unsatisfied—
      the story came to an end without ending.
All the innumerable, unfinished incidents,
    the prematurely: torn-off buds,
    the unknown lives, the dust of common fame,
      so many ideas, so many fears and blunders—
day and night and in all directions in life
    these are all falling down in endless torrents.
Fleeting tears, fleeting smiles
    are falling in heaps;
      I hear their sounds constantly.
All these neglected things,
    all these momentary joys and pleasures
      I pile up around me;
With them I create an oblivion rainfall
    of my life's Sraban nights.

HING TING CHHAT
A DREAM EPIC

One night King Habuchandra dreamt a dream,
    Pondering over it, Gabuchandra was silent.
It seemed that three monkeys were sitting
    near his head, appreciatively picking lice.
If he but moved a bit, they slapped him,
    His eyes and face bore marks of scratching.
Suddenly they disappeared
    and a gypsy showed up;
He began to lament, saying,
    "The bird has flown away !"
Spotting the king before him,
    he put him on his shoulder,
      then sat him hanging on a high perch.

Beneath him a decrepit old hag had fun,
    tickling his feet and laughing her head off.
The king moaned, "What misery!"
    No one released him,
        He tried to raise his feet but couldn't.
The king flapped his arms like a bird,
    The gypsy whispered "Hing ting chhat."
The words of the Dream Epic are like nectar,
    The poet Gourananda narrates,
        The pious listen.

In the kingdom of Habupur for six-seven days
    all eyes are sleepless, stomachs are empty.
Throughout the land young and old are agitated
    as they ponder,
        their palms against withered cheeks,
            their heads leaning forward.
Boys forget their games, pundits their books,
    girls keep quiet; there's such a crisis!
Sitting in rows, they remain speechless;
    The more they become worried,
        the lower their heads tilt forward, downward
            as if studying mushrooms
                on the ground,
        as if all were sitting to a formless feast.
Once in a while they let out deep sighs,
    Suddenly they all shout 'Hing ting chhat'.
The words of the Dream Epic are like nectar,
    The poet Gourananda narrates,
        The virtuous listen.

From all directions came groups of pundits;
    the girdled, the unconquerables and others.
From Ujjoyini came the learned Abatangsha
    of the family of the nephew
        of the great poet Kalidash.
They took out voluminous books and turned the
                          pages,

Tufts of uncut hair flew
    while they often shook their heads.
When they shook their massive heads
    it seemed like a ripe grain field
        with the tips swaying in the breeze.
One after another they consulted the Vedas,
    law books, mythologies, grammars, dictionaries,
Nowhere and in no way did they find the meaning,
    They increased in heaps
        the letters of the spirants and nasals.
Silently they sit; There's a critical situation—
    Occasionally there's a shout of 'Hing ting chhat'.
The words of the Dream Epic are like nectar,
    The poet Gourananda narrates,
        The virtuous listen.

Giving up, King Habuchandra announced:
    "I hear there is a community of learned men
        in the land of Mlechchha.
    Call them here no matter where they may be,
        They may be able to find out the meaning."
The non Hindu pundits came,
    brown-haired, blue-eyed, pale-yellow cheeked;
        Drums beat, tomtoms beat.
They came wearing black jackets,
    thick but trim.
Their irritation increased with the summer heat,
    O how fierce looking they became!
Without any introduction they took out their
        watches and said,
"We have only seventeen minutes left;
    If you have anything to say, say it quickly!"
Everyone in the assembly chanted
    "Hing ting chhat!"
The words of the Dream Epic are like nectar,
    the poet Gourananda narrates,
        The virtuous listen.

Hearing about the dream,
    the Mlechchha faces turned brilliant red,
Fire blazed in their faces and eyes,
    Striking their right hands against
        their left palms, they exclaimed angrily:
"You asked us to come here,
    Then why this huge joke?"
A French pundit was present there;
    His face brightened by a smile,
        he folded his arms across his chest,
            and, with his head inclined, said:
"What I have come to know about the dream
    is really fit for a king.
It is not everyone's luck to have such a dream.
    Yet, I suppose, that a dream is nothing
        but a dream, even though it got a place
            in the king's head.
If you want money, there's lots of it
    in the royal treasury.
What about the dream? There's no meaning to it
    no matter how much we beat our heads.
Again, there's no meaning, but I tell you frankly,
    O how sweet it is to hear "Hing ting chhat!"
The words of the Dream Epic are like nectar,
    The poet Gourananda narrates,
        The virtuous listen.

On hearing this, they all shrieked:
    "Shame on you! You ought to be ashamed!
        Where did this utterly stupid, heretical
            unbeliever come from!
How can we accept 'the dream is only
    a dream, an aberration of the brain'!
We are a world-famous race,
    regarding religion as dear as life!
'Ignore the dream'?
    This is robbery at high noon!"

Red-eyed, King Habuchandra said,
"Gabuchandra, let them be taught a good lesson !
　　Put thorns on top of them !
　　　Put thorns under them !
　　　　Distribute them among the greyhounds."
Inside of seventeen minutes
　　there was no trace of the Mlechcha pundits.
Everyone in the assembly wept for joy,
　　Peace returned again to this holy state.
Defiantly setting their faces and eyes,
　　the pundits again took up
　　　their singsong chant: "Hing ting chhat."
The words of the Dream Epic are like nectar,
　　the poet Gourananda narrates,
　　　the virtuous listen.

From ancient Bengal there came in the meantime
　　the disciples of foreign pundits
　　　who excelled their teachers.
Bareheaded, unadorned, unashamed of their
　　　　　　　　　　　　　scanty dress,
　　their loin clothes were always working loose.
Their bodies were so lean and short
　　that there was doubt about their very existence
　　　until words came out of them.
All were amazed to hear such loud sounds come
　　out of such small instruments.
They knew nought of common courtesies,
　　They wished no one well,
They became furious
　　if anyone asked them their fathers' names.
Haughtily they demanded,
　　"What s the arguing about ?
Once we hear what it's all about,
　　we can decide it in a few words;
　　　We can explain it in contradictory terms."
In a show of solidarity

they all shouted together: "Wing ting chhat !"
The words of the Dream Epic are like nectar,
　　The poet Gourananda narrates,
　　　　The virtuous listen.

A holy man from ancient Bengal, on hearing
　　about the dream, set his face solemnly
　　　　and spoke for three hours,
"The meaning is exceedingly simple
　　and quite clear; it's a very old idea,
　　　　but newly discovered."
The three eyes of Shiva,
　　the three ages collectively,
　　　　the three characteristics of primal
　　　　　　qualities of men and creatures,
the differences between persons according
　　to power is doubly corrupted.
All the evolution, revolution, polarization,
　　the power of life, the power of Shiva
　　　　make everything discordant.
Attraction, repulsion, the nature of man
　　are shaped or decomposed by
　　　　molecular attraction.
Sentient electricity flowing at the tip
　　of kush (grass) exemplifies the concept
　　　　of primal force.
The three powers in the three states
　　of nature are clearly shown as illusions.
　　　　To say it briefly: "Hing ting chhat !"
The words of the Dream Epic are like nectar,
　　The poet Gourananda narrates.
　　　　The pious listen.

The whole area shook with the roar
　　of 'Excellent ! Excellent ! Excellent !'
One and all said, 'It's clear-quite clear !
　　All that had been hard to understand

      is now as clear as water,
          as clear as the empty sky.'
Heaving a sigh of relief, the king stood up,
     From his head he removed his crown
       and put it on the head of the slender Bengali.
         His head seemed ready to fall off
           with its burden.
After a long time all anxiety had disappeared,
     After a long involvement the land of Habu
       began to show signs of normal life.
Children began to play again,
     Old men began to smoke again,
       In an instant women began to talk again,
The country-wide headache went away in an instant,
     They all understood 'Hing ting chhat'.
The words of the Dream Epic are like nectar,
     The poet Gourananda narrates,
       The pious listen.

Whoever hears this recitation of the Dream Epic
    will have all his wrong notions removed,
      He won't think otherwise.
No one will be deceived into thinking
    that the world is a world.
In a flash he'll see
    that the truth is a lie.
Whatever is, is not !
    Whatever is not is,
      All this will be bright and vivid.
He will add his own interpretation
    to whatever everyone thinks about anything
      after simple consideration.
Come on, friends ! Let out a yawn,
    Stretch out on your backs.
In this uncertain world
    this much is certain:
In this world everything is false
    all is illusive,

Only the dream is real,
> Nothing else is real.
The words of the Dream Epic are like nectar,
> the poet Gourananda narrates
>> The pious listen.

TOUCHSTONE

A madman was searching constantly
> for the touchstone.
The matted hair on his head was brownish
> with dust and mud,
>> Like a dark shadow was his body.
Compressing his lips
> and closing the door of his heart, day and night
>> he enkindled in his eyes an intense flame.
His eyes seemed ever to be searching for something
> just like the firefly of the night
>> searches with its own light.
He had no food or shelter,
> He smeared dust and ashes on his body.
Only a gray loin cloth was wound round his waist,
> There was no one in the world he could talk with.
Poorer and lowlier than a street beggar,
> yet he had such pride;
Gold and silver he despised,
> He was not envious of riches—
Seeing his condition, I was inclined to laugh,
> He wants full possession of the touchstone,
>> He wants nothing more.

Up ahead there was the roaring of the sea,
> deep and shoreless.
Waves rose up one after another,
> beside themselves with laughter
>> at the sight of the bizarre activities
>>> of the madman.

The sky stared with a steadfast look,
    The moaning wind blew freely.
At dawn the sun climbed toward the forehead
    of the eastern sky,
In the evening
    the moon rose slowly.
Incessant streams of water babbled sweetly
    as if they longed to tell some deep mysteries,
It seemed as though they knew everything,
    including the site of the longed for treasure,
Anyone who understood that language
    could seek and find it.
The sea itself was listening to its own voice,
    narrating a great ballad, ignoring all else.
People came and went, wept and laughed,
    On the shore the madman was engaged
    in search of the touchstone.

One day long ago, it is said,
    a testing streak of gold appeared, only that;
    The first act of creation
        was revealed in the sky.
Seized with curiosity,
    all the gods and demons came on tiptoe
    to this seashore.
Bending their heads forward,
    they remained standing silently,
        looking firmly toward the boundless sea.
Motionless for a long time, they closed their eyes
    and heard the eternal song of the great ocean.
After that, out of curiosity,
    they jumped into the fathomless water
    and churned up this endless mystery.
After a long period of distress
    they observed the goddess Lakshmi,
She appeared in this world
    as unparalleled beauty.

Lean-limbed and clothed in a piece of rag,
    the madman was constantly searching
        for the touchstone on that same shore.

After many days, I suppose, he gave up hope,
    though he moved about, searching.
He didn't know how to rest,
    He had lost all hope,
        but not the habit of searching.
During the whole night a separated bird
    was calling on some tree,
        but the luckless one didn't find his mate,
Day and night, nevertheless, he called,
    hopelessly, untiringly,
His only activity was to keep on calling,
    sleeplessly.
Nobody knows whom the ocean wants
    as it forgets all other activity
        and constantly throws up huge waves sky ward.
No matter how much it moaned,
    it never got anyone,
Still it raised its arms toward the sky,
    Such was its vow,
Seeking someone in the sky,
    the entire universe tries endlessly
        and with all its might,
            taking the stars and planets with it.
In the same way,
    with dusty, long and matted hair,
        the frenzied one was engaged on the shore
            in his search for the touchstone.

One day a village boy said to him,
    "O guru master, what's this ?
        What's that, that I see round your waist ?
        Where did you get the golden chain ?
The begging ascetic was amazed,
    The chain indeed was gold;

Without his knowledge
    the iron had changed into gold.
What a marvel !
    He took it off and kept staring at it.
      He rubbed his eyes,
        No, it wasn't a dream.
Striking his forehead, he sat on the ground
    severely to berate and reproach himself.
Staring ahead madly, he wonders:
    Alas ! Alas ! Where did it go ?
      The desired success had escaped him
        after coming within reach.
Out of habit he gathered a lot of stones
    and struck them against the chain,
      raising light clattering sounds.
Never did he look at them,
    He threw them far away—
      and one of them was the touchstone.

The fading sun was about to set,
    The sky was golden, the ocean liquid gold,
      The goddess of the western sky
        had a golden dream.
The ascetic-beggar returned to his previous path
    to seek again the lost gem.
His old strength is gone,
    He stoops under the load of his body,
      His heart sank like a felled tree.
The long, old path lay lifeless before him,
    How much farther ? There's no end in sight.
On all sides the desert sands burned fiercely,
    The whole land was gloomy
      in the shade of oncoming night.
After seeking for half his life,
    he had been able to touch it
      for a fleeting moment.
Now he offered the remaining half of his broken life
    in search of the touchstone.

A VAISNAB POEM

Vaisnab songs are only for Boikuntha,
    the celestial abode of Vishnu !
The amorous attractions, the courtships,
    the attachments, the pique and sensitiveness,
      the love trysts, the dalliance,
        the separation and union of lovers,
    the songs of Brindaban, the dreams of love
      on a Sraban night on the bank of the
        River Kalinda, the meetings face to face
          at the foot of the kadamba tree,
        displays of shyness and apprehension—

Are these only for God !
    Are these streams of love songs not meant
      to assuage the intense thirst for love,
        day and night, of men and women,
          the afficted dwellers of this earth ?

In this song festival !
    there exist only He and the devotee
      in blissful solitude,
If we men and women, standing outside,
    listen eagerly to a few tunes of that song,
If we hear the tunes from a distance,
    in fresh youth, in a new spring,
      the heart thrills with delight—
If we hear those tunes unexpectedly from a distance
    we see our world twice as beautiful—
Charming and delightful become the river
    that speeds in our forest shades
      and the kadamba tree that blossoms
        near our cottages in the rainy season—
If, touched by that love-afflicated tune,
    I turn around and see the one person
      that I love on this earth standing beside me
        holding my hand, inclining her heart
      toward me, offering her own silent love,

if, in that song, she finds her own feelings expressed,
if the full light of love
    blossoms out on her face,
        then, friend of His, what is it to you ?
            who is harmed by that ?

Oh Vaisnab poet, tell me the truth,
    Where did you get this glow of love ?
        Where did you learn that love song
            so stricken with separation ?
Whose eyes inspired you to remember
    the tearful eyes of Radhika ?
Who embraced you,
    who submerged you in the fathomless sea
        of her heart in the trysting bed
            one lonely spring night ?
From whose face and eyes did you steal
    such words of love,
        the intense, heart-rendering eagerness
            of Radhika ? Now she has no right
                to that song !
For ever will you deprive her
    of the expression of the sentiments
        stored in her woman's heart !

In the gardens near our bungalows flowers bloom,
    Some lay these at God's feet,
        Some keep them for their loved one
            God is not displeased with that.
These garlands of love songs are strung
    for the trysts of men and women;
        Some give them to Him,
            Some garland their loved ones.
What we can give to God
    we give to our loved one,
        What we can give to our loved one
            we give to God.

> Where can we get more !
> We make God our beloved,
> We make our beloved God.

So many gifts of love strung by the Vaisnab poet
   are winging their way up the Boikuntha path,
In the middle of that path
   men and women are snatching away,
  as much as they can, that imperishable nectar
   for their own dear cottages.
In this world, age after age, at all times
   youthful boys and girls, mature men and women
     have been so fickle
       in their inclinations and actions.
Persons in both groups have lost their self-control,
   They are imprudent and unthinking.
They are the ravagers of beauty, of loveliness,
   They want to loot everything.
So many songs, so much rhythm,
   so much love bursting with emotion—
    so much delight—
      all this is flowing past their doors,
So they have all come
   to mingle with that stream of nectar
     amid a sweet, soft murmur of pleasure.
Those seafarers fill their pitchers
   from the stream of love and take them
     for themselves to their own cottages
  on the shore, having made no judgement at all.
O righteous pundit,
   falsely you find fault with them,
     falsely you burn with rage.
The One who owns all this wealth
   is smiling a smile of boundless tenderness
     with endless satisfaction.

TWO BIRDS

A captive bird was in a golden cage,
    A wild bird was in the forest.
No one knows how they met,
    No one knows what was in the mind
        of Providence.
The wild bird said,
    'O friend caged bird, 'Let's go to the forest.'
The caged bird said, 'O wild bird friend,
    let's stay in the cage in solitude.'
The wild bird said, 'No ! Never !
    I'll not let myself be enchained.'
The caged bird said, 'Alas ! How can I
    get out and go to the forest ?'

Sitting outside, the wild bird sang
    all the songs of the forest;
The imprisoned bird recited
    all the sounds it had been taught.
        O how their languages differed !
The wild bird said, 'O caged friend,
    let me hear you sing the songs of the forest.'
The imprisoned bird said, 'O wild friend,
    learn the songs of the cage.'
The forest bird replied, 'No ! Never !
    I want no songs that have been taught !'
The imprisoned bird said. 'Alas !
    How can I ever sing the songs of the forest !'

The forest bird remarked, 'The sky is deep blue;
    there are no obstructions anywhere.'
The pet bird responded, 'Oh how neatly
    the cage is screened on all sides.'
The wild bird said,
    'Free yourself completely in the clouds.'
The captive bird said,
    'Restrain yourself in solitary comfort.'

The forest bird, said, 'No ! never !
    Where will I find space to fly ?'
The caged bird remarked, 'Alas !
    In the clouds where is there a place to sit ?'

In this way the two birds loved each other,
    though they could not come close together,
Through the gaps in the cage they touched
    each other with their beaks;
        Silently they regarded each other.
Neither one could understand the other
    nor could they make themselves understood.
Each one flapped its wings,
    In great distress they cried, 'Come closer !'
The wild bird said, 'No ! never !
    When will you overcome
        the obstructions of the cage ?'
The imprisoned bird remarked,
    'Alas ! I have no strength to fly.'

MOON IN THE SKY

The only thing he kept saying was:
    'Give me the moon !'
Days and nights slipped by,
    He holds up his arms and weeps.
The sky is laughing, the breeze is blowing,
    the birds are singing happily.
Herdsmen go to the fields at dawn,
    In the evening they are homeward bound.
Boys and girls, brothers and sisters
    are playing in a corner of the courtyard.
A mother smiles to herself as she gazes
    at the infant in her arms.
Some people go to market, some go down the path;
    All are busy with their own work.

O how much hearsay,
    O how much noise rises to the sky !
Wayfarers ask him, 'Who are you weeping so ?'
    Eyes filled with tears, he keeps saying,
      'I have not yet got the moon.'

Morning and evening
    unasked – for flowers fall into his lap.
The southern breeze brushes his forehead
    with an affectionate hand.
The morning light touches his body in blessing.
    The night covers him with her anchal
      in silent affection.
A child, wanting to be fondled,
    comes up to him and embraces him warmly.
A young man, comes to his side
    and wants to make him his friend.
In this home by the path
    there is so much coming and going,
      so much love and devotion.
So much earthly life happiness
    comes very close to him and drifts away.
With face averted and eyes full of tears,
    he just sits there and keeps saying,
      'I don't want any of you;
      I only want the moon.'

The moon stayed where it was.
    He too remained in the same place.
At last, when his days were numbered,
    he suddenly thought of something;
      He turned round and gazed about—
He saw that the green earth was beautiful
    on the shore of the blue sea.
A farmer was reaping paddy in a golden field;
    With sails raised, small boats moved along,
      while the boatmen squatted and sang.

Bells were ringing in a far-off temple.
    Women were going to the ghat to get water.
        By village paths men were going to market.
Heaving a sigh, he said, with a heavy heart,
    'I don't want the moon
        if I can get back this life.'

He saw the beautiful village full of life,
    ever noisy with daily joys and sorrows.
With the nectar of tenderness
    the mistress was moving about her home,
        sweetening every day with her daily work.
Morning and evening
    the two brothers come like dutiful sons.
The night took everyone into her lap
    and closed her eyes.
Tiny flowers, flitting smiles, trifling remarks,
    fleeting joys, the loves of every moment,
        cheerful faces—why these are all
            blossoming out spontaneously
                around the life of man !
Sitting on a solitary mountain peak,
    he reviewed all these over and over.

He sees
    in the distance the lines of his past life
        like a shady palace limned in new colours
        with the rays of the setting sun.
Those whom he had never wanted to see again
    began to appear with a new lustre
        on the shore of his sea of memory.
A purabee tune was playing dolefully
    in his despondent heart ;
He extended his arms,
    desperately wanting to go back to that life.
The light of day had disappeared;
    Still he stayed on, looking back.

Now he wanted to get
    all that had been within his reach,
      nothing more.
A happy and prosperous life had been abandoned;
    No one knows where he went.
Did he go to lament for the moon
    where there was no moon, no sun ?

BREAK IN THE SONG

Kashinath, a modern young man, is singing,
    filling the assembly hall with tunes.
The seven notes of the scale are playing
    in his throat like seven pets.
His voice, like a sharp sword
    is dancing around in all ten directions.
His voice is sparking like lightning.
    It doesn't know where and when it should go.
The voice itself creates an illusion of danger.
    Then it chops up the danger.
The people in the assembly are speechless.
    In praise they keep saying 'Wow ! Wow !'

Only the aged King Pratap Roy is sitting woodenly,
    No songs does he like except Barajlal's,
All his life he passed listening to his songs—
    so many songs of clouds on rainy days,
      so many kafi on days of Holi !
He sang agaman songs on autumn morns,
    He sang bijoya songs—
His heart would be seized with emotion,
    His eyes would be filled with tears.
When friends met together,
    the assembly hall would be full—
      He sang about the milkmaids of Gokul
        in bhoopali and multani tunes.

Often he came to homes on wedding nights,
>   Red clothes were worn by the servants,
>   > Hundreds of lamps would burn.
The new bridegroom sat with a bashful face,
>   wearing ornaments studded with gems,
>   > Friends of the same age joked with him.
Sitting before the king,
>   Barajlal took up a shahana tune.
Pratap Roy's heart was full
>   of all those days, of all those songs.
Listening to the songs of anyone else
>   did not touch the royal heart,
His old vigour, it seemed, did not wake up in
>   > his heart
>   because of the force of the old spell.
So Pratap Roy just looked on,
>   Uselessly Kashi shook his head;
One after another the tunes came,
>   In their hearts they found no response.
When the songs finally stopped,
>   old Kashinath wanted to rest for a while,
With a mocking smile the king looked toward
>   > Barjalal—
>   Putting his mouth to his ear,
he said, 'Honourable Virtuoso,
>   let's hear some real music.
>   > Do they call that music ?
It sounds like a hunting cat
>   fooling around with a bird.
In the old days those were songs,
>   Today no attention is paid to songs.'
Old Barajlal, gray-haired and white-turbaned,
>   bowed to the assembly and slowly took his seat.
With his vein-revealing left hand
>   he took up the tanpura,
Eyes closed and head bent over,
>   he began an imankallan air.

Trembling, the feeble voice died out
    in a corner of the vast room
just as a little bird cannot fly in a storm
    though it tries with all its might.
Pratap Roy, sitting at his left
    kept encouraging him—
Into his ear he kept whispering,
    'Ah ! Oh ! Sing out ! Sing out !'
One and all in the assembly were inattentive—
    Some whispered, some yawned, some went
                                   home.
Some called the servants, yelling,
    'Hey there ! Bring me tobacco and betel leaf.'
Others fanned themselves and remarked,
    'Gosh ! It's hot today.'
The busy ones were coming and going;
    No longer was there a semblance of quiet—
Silent had been the assembly,
    Now noise approached a crescendo.
Into it sank the old man's song
    just as a frail boat sinks in a violent storm;
One could only see his fingers
    wildly trembling on the tanpura.
In his heart, from where the song came,
    his own happiness welled up
while the tumult of disdain, like a stone,
    pressed down on that fountain head.
Where is the song ? where is its life ?
    They went off in different directions.
Still Baraj sang heart and soul
    just to please his master.
How had one line of the song got lost ?
    What was wrong ?
Quickly he tried again,
    He sought to correct it.
Yet again he forgot,
    He just couldn't recall it,
        In shame, he shook his head;

He began to sing again,
    Again he forgot the line and stopped !
His hands trembled twice as violently,
    Then he remembered his guru.
His voice quavered in distress
    like a lamp about to go out.
Dropping the lines of the song,
    he retained only the tune,
Suddenly he started wailing in distress,
    Each effort to sing produced only wailing.
Where into the distance had the tunes gone,
    Where had the musical measures drifted away;
The string of song tore
    and pearls of tears fell off.

His shamed head he laid on the tanpura,
    the friend of his childhood—
Having forgotten practised songs,
    he could recall only the tearful ballads
        of childhood.
His eyes brimming with tears,
    Pratap Roy caressed him,
With compassionate love, in a doleful voice
    he said, 'Come on. Let's go away from here.'
They left the hall of ceremonies
    burning with hundreds of lamps
        like so many glowing eyes.
Out went the two old friends,
    holding hands.

Baraj said, hands folded respectfully before him,
    'Master, our assembly has broken up.
Now is the time for newcomers,
    for new entertainments in this world.'
On this earth
    only you and I will have our solitary assembly.
Don't bring a new audience,
    I earnestly entreat you, master.

A song is not only for the singer,
    Two people have to blend together in harmony.
One will sing full-throatedly,
    The other will sing to himself.
Waves of water strike the heart of the shore,
    Then sweet notes appear,
In the wind the forest shudders and trembles,
    Then the rustling of leaves is heard.
On earth, wherever there is sound,
    it comes from the interaction of two things first.
Where there is no love,
    there is a mute, a dumb assembly.

I WON'T LET YOU GO

The horse carriage is ready at the door;
    Now it's noon, an autumn noon;
        The sunshine is becoming extremely hot,
Dust fills the air on the empty village path;
    After spreading out her ragged clothes,
        a tired old beggar woman is sleeping
            in the cool shade of a fig tree
                while the midday breeze is blowing;
It seems like a nightfull of burning sunshine,
    It's hushing everything, everyone,
        for on all sides it's silent and still—
            Only in my home is there no restful sleep.

The month of Ashin has gone by;
    After the puja vacation
        I'll have to go to a far-off place
            where work awaits me.
Bustling about,
    the servants are tying up my bags and bundles.
In the rooms
    There's constant shouting and calling.

The mistress of the house, with tearful eyes,
   is suffering the weight of stone
      on her heart;
         Yet, there's no time to spare for weeping;
She's moving about anxiously,
   looking after preparations for my departure;
She pays no heed
   to the mounting load of things to take.
I exclaim, 'What's going on here ?
   So many pitchers, pots, jars, plates,
      bottles, boxes,
         so much clothes and bedding ?
            I'll take some of these and leave the rest.'
No one pays the least attention to me.
   'Who knows if you'll need this or that;
     Then where will you get these things
        in a far off place ?—
  yellow pigeon-pea, fine rice, betel-nut and
  pan leaves, some lumps of datepalm treacle,
    ripe and hardened coconut,
       two pots of good mustard oil,
         cakes of dried mango juice,
        dried slices of mango,
           about two quarts of milk;
  those glass phials and small containers
   hold some medicines,
  there are some sweets in that pot—
    For love of me, don't forget to eat.'
    I realized it was useless to argue
The load was piled up in heaps
   like a high mountain.
I glanced at the clock,
   then turned and looked at the face
     of my loved one;
Softly I said, 'Well then, I'm going.'
   Just then she turned her face aside
     and, looking down, covered her eyes

with the end of her sari
to hide the tears-of-misfortune.

Outside, near the door,
   my four-year old daughter is sitting absent
                                    mindedly,
By this time on any other day
   she would have finished her bath,
Her eyelids would have been closed in sleep
   before taking her noon rice;
      Today her mother pays no attention to her;
         The morning is going by without her
            eating or bathing.
All this while she is hovering near me
   like a shadow,
      staring steadily at the preparations
      for my departure.
Who knows what she's thinking now
   while she's sitting silently outside,
      her little body tired and exhausted.
When I said 'Darling, I'm going,'
   sne responded, sad-eyed and pale-faced,
      'I won't let you go.'
She remained where she was,
   she didn't take hold of my hand,
      She didn't close the door;
She only made known her heart's claim-of-love:
   'I won't let you go.'
But, alas ! Time was up,
She had to let me go.

Oh my simple daughter, who are you ?
   Where did you get such strength so as to say
      so boldly, 'I won't let you go' ?
Oh proud one, in this world whom can you
                                    hold back
   with your two tiny hands ?

With whom will you fight
  as you sit at the door of the house,
    only using your tired and small body
      and that bit of a heart full of love ?
In this world only from a heart distressed
  through fear and shyness
    can we express the wishes
      of our inmost feelings,
  Only we can say,
    'We have no desire to leave.'
  Who can say such words,
    'I won't let you go !'
On hearing this proud message of your powerful love
  from your childish mouth,
    I was amusedly drawn to earthly life;
You, the defeated one, eyes filled with tears,
  just remain, like a picture,
    sitting by the door—
After looking long at you, I went away,
  wiping my tears.

While going, I saw on both sides of the road
  the paddy of autumn bent low
    with its load of grain and basking in the sun.
The listless trees that line the road
  spend the whole day looking at their own
                                    shadows.
The brimming Ganges of autumn is flowing swiftly;
  Spotless cloudlets are lying on the sky
    like new-born calves, soft and tender,
      sleeping peacefully, sated with mother-milk.
I sigh as I view the earth spreading to the horizon,
  lying uncovered in the bright sunshine,
    age-after-age weary.

What great sadness overwhelms the whole sky.
    the whole earth !

No matter how far I go,
    I hear but one heart-rending melody:
        'I'll not let you go.'
From the ends of the earth
    to the last shore of the blue sky
        there eternally resounds:
            'I'll not let you go ! I'll not let you go !'
Everything says, 'I won't let you go !'
    Even though grass is a trifling thing,
        yet Mother Earth clasps it to her bosom
        and says with all her might:
            'I'll not let you go !'
The flame of the flickering lamp is about to go out.
    but something is holding it back
        from the edge of darkness
        and says a hundred times: 'I'll not
                      let you go !'
In the whole universe
  and pervading heaven and earth,
      the oldest utterance, the deepest wailing is:
        'I'll not let you go !'
Alas ! Still we have to part,
    Still we have to go away.
        This has been going on from time
                      immemorial !
In the stream of creation
    conveyed by the ocean of the universal
                      cata-clysm
        all went off whizzing with intense speed,
        with eager, extended arms,
            calling out 'I'll not let you go,'
    and filling the shore of the universe
    with a grief-stricken uproar.
The waves in back call out to those in front:
    'I'll not let you go, I'll not let you go !'
        No one pays attention to that,
            Nobody gives a response.

Incessantly and from all sides I hear
    that heart-breaking,
        that doleful wailing of the universe
            in the cry of my daughter.
The foolish outburst of the universe
    is like that of the child.
It for ever loses all that it gets,
    Still its grip does not slacken;
Unceasingly it still says 'I won't let you go'
    like that four-year old daughter
        with the pride of unabating love.
Her face is pale, her eyes are full of tears,
    At every moment her pride is shattered;
Still her love never accepts defeat,
    Still her love says in a choked voice:
        'I'll not let you go !'
The more she is overcome, the more she says,
    'The one I love can never go away from me !
        Is there anything at all in the universe
            so extremely distressed,
                so greater-than-all, so overwhelming
                      as my desire !'
Proudly saying this, she proclaims :
    'I'll not let you go !'
In an instant she sees her love's treasure disappear
    like dry, worthless dust:
Her eyes are suffused with tears;
    Her inclined head, shorn of glory,
        falls to the earth like an uprooted tree.
Still love says,
    'God will never allow trust to be broken.
        I have His solemn promise signed by Himself,
            a document of eternal title'—
So, with chest thrust out this wisp of a child,
    so soft, so delicate, so slender,
        faces all-powerful Death and says,
            'Oh Death, you don't exist !'—

Such proud words!
          Death just sits and laughs.
That immortal love, afflicted by death,
     covers this endless world
          like the tears over the doleful eyes,
               ever trembling with perplexed dread.
Hopeless tired hope spreads a mist of melancholy
     that pervades the world.
          It seem to me that I can see it today—
Two foolish arms in a fruitless embrace
     try to enclose the universe silently, sorrowfully,
In the water of the restless stream
     there is an unwavering reflection;
          It, is the illusion of clouds
               full of tear-rain.

Today I hear such agitation
     in the rustling of the trees;
The lazy, listless noonday breeze
     is playing in vain with the dry leaves:
The day is slowly ending,
     lengthening its shadow under the fig tree.
It seems as if the eternal flute is wailing
     in a rural tune at the edge of the universe;
Hearing it,
     the listless earth remains sitting
          with dishevelled hair
               in the far-reaching rice field
                    on the shore of the Ganges,
                         pulling over her bosom
                              a yellow-gold anchal of sunshine;
She is gazing fixedly at the far-off blue sky,
     speechless, wordless—
I have seen that pale face of hers—
     like that of my four-year old daughter
          at the side of the door:
               absorbed, dazed, deeply hurt.

TO THE OCEAN
ON VIEWING THE BAY OF BENGAL OFF PURI

Oh ocean, primordial mother, the earth,
   your only daughter, is on your lap,
      so there is no drowsiness in your eyes,
so fears, forever, hope forever,
   agitation forever pervade your bosom,
so in the perpetual song of blessing spreading
                          everywhere
   there are sounds like the Vedic mantras
      in the continuous, tranquil sky,
         voicing the endless prayer of the heart,
            toward the temple of Indra,
so endless times you kiss the sleeping earth,
   embracing her whole body,
      binding her with bonds of waves,
         covering her soft body carefully,
            artistically, lovingly with your blue anchal.

Oh ocean, deceptively displaying feigned neglect,
   you slowly advance on tiptoe,
      then you withdraw a great distance
         as if you want to abandon her;
Singing a joyful tune, you return delightedly
   and jump on her bosom in roaring waves;
      with lots of bright laughter, with tears,
         with loving, prideful happiness you wet
            the unblemished forehead of the earth
               with blessings.
Ever moved is your great heart,
   completely full of affection—
Where is the source, where is the end of this
                              affection !
   Where is the bottom ! Where are the shores !
Tell me
   who can understand her profound peace,

          her limitless eagerness, her profound silence,
            he all-pervading babbling,
              her laughter, her tears !
At times it seems you cannot control yourself;
        You mad one, with your breasts swelling
          with affection, you dash off and clasp
            the earth to your bosom
              in a fierce outburst of passion.
Trembling because of your furious torment,
      the earth wants to scream with suppressed
                                breath,
Like a demoness
  you bind, oppress and shake her
    in frenzied love-hunger
      as if, shattering her completely
        in your infinite insatiety,
          you want to devour and destroy her
            in monstrous annihilation.
Slowly dawn comes
  and casts a calm look at you.
Friend, evening lovingly comforts you
  with her affectionate touch
    then silently goes into the temple of darkness.
Night, like an intimate friend,
  listens to your heart-rending weeping
    overflowing with suppressed repentance.

I am a child of the earth,
  sitting on your shore, listening to your sounds.
I keep thinking:
  it seems as if I can understand
    some of its meaning;
      It's like the language
        that a dumb person uses with relatives,
It seems as though
  the blood that flows in the chambers
    of my heart knows this language;
      it learned nothing else.

It seems as though I remember
  when I was absorbed in the unborn fetus
    in your huge womb,
    then for endless ages your constant billowing
      was stamped on my whole heart,
When I lower my eyes
  while sitting on the solitary shore,
    I hear that old, limpid murmur of the waves,
Then the memory of my former birth
  and the eternal throbbing of life
    in your motherly heart on the earth
      lying in your womb
        awakes in all my veins
          like a very weak glow.
Then, age after age, from one direction to another,
  you were alone, undivided, shoreless
    and beside yourself with joy
    without understanding the fathomless mystery
    of the first pregnancy.
Day and night your empty, childless heart
  was worried with a mysterious, loving anxiety,
    with amorous feelings, with an unnoticed,
      wonderful, possessive attachment,
        with secret longing.
Every morning dawn used to come and try to guess
  the birthday of this great child.
Every night the stars remained gazing
  unblinkingly at the childless bed.
The profound love-restlessness
  of the primeval mother, childless, creatureless,
that wakeful longing
  full of imminent expectation,
that unknown ache in your boundless heart
  for the great future—
all these are awaking constantly in my heart
  like the memories of different ages.
Such secret pains. such unknown desires
  for the unseen and the far-off

are also arousing rustling sounds in my heart.
It seems as if new continents are being created
  at every moment in the ocean of the human heart;
    Mankind itself is not aware of this.
Even a partial perception of this
  makes a person restless;
This vague feeling has infused in man's heart
  tremendous hope without form, without satiety.
    Its abode is beyond proof, beyond perception.
Logic makes fun of it,
  but man's inmost feellings know it is so.
Though there are innumerable obstacles,
  mankind never doubts,
    just as a mother knows
      the hidden child in her womb,
        when affection arises in her heart,
        when her breasts fill with milk.
I am gazing at you with that hope,
  full of life, speechless, perplexed.
You, oh sea, with a huge laugh, are drawing
    my inmost heart at great speed
      into your waves
        as though I am a mere infant.
Oh ocean, can you understand
  this human language of mine?
Do you know
  that the surface of this earth of yours
    is now afflicted with distress,
      turning this side and that side,
        eyes pouring out tears,
          frequently exhaling her hot breath.
She doesn't know what she wants,
  She doesn't know how to quench her thirst.
Mentally she has lost the means
  of ascertaining the right way
    through aberration's net of illusion.
Speak to her new and amazing words of comfort,

like the grave and sonorous sounds
    of the monsoon clouds,
        from your extremely deep heart,
Stroking her worry-heated forehead
    repeatedly and rhythmically
        with your cool motherly hand,
lovingly kiss her whole body over and over
    and say to her, 'Peace ! Peace !'
        Say to her, 'Sleep ! Sleep !'

AWAITING

Oh Death.
    I know you have set up your dwelling
        in my heart.
Where, in the solitary bower there blooms
    all my love and affection,
    the desires of my secret heart,
    the sadness and happiness of my life,
    the pain of my inmost heart,
    all my longings and accomplishments
        limned by the marks
            of the smiles and tears of my whole life—
where, in the shadow of paradise
    there interplays without diffidence
        the wealth of my heart,
        the idols of my affection,
        the memories of my whole life,
        the rays of delight—
O how much light, O how much shade,
    how varied the songs of tiny birds—
Oh Death, I now realize
    that you have come among all these
        and have set up your dwelling.

Day and night, constantly
    there is interplay throughout the world.
        Life is restless.

I see that all the wayfarers are going
    along the highway in untiring movement—
Birds are flying livelily in the blue sky
    made pale by the sunlight,
At daybreak fresh flowers are blooming
    in the forest set a trembling by the breeze—
On all sides, at dawn, at eventide
    oh how countless are the contacts among people
      oh how endless is the coming and going,
At every dawning
    the days start new chapters of life—
Day and night only you stay sitting in a corner,
    staring ahead with a blank look,
Now and then at night you flap your wings—
    My heart throbs.
Have you brought some new message, some
                 setter news
    from that realm on the other shore
      of the distant sea from where you have come?
There, on the silent shore,
    the billows are beating in most solemn tones
      as they keep musical rhythm.
How are you able to make that sound play
    in my small heart!
On the shore of the cage of my heart
    day and night there is this incessant throbbing
      of the endless waves pounding
        in solemn and perfect time,
          No one hears this.
The trifling songs of my heart,
    the sweet, soft notes of my love—
who has introduced into their midst
    the Bhairab songs of the endless sea!

You must surely love this life-bird
    dwelling in my heart,
That's why you are sitting at its side
    and very slowly drawing closer and closer!

Ardently, silently you are straining,
    gazing intently into its eyes day and night,
Sitting motionless you are worshipping Rudra
    attentively, zealously.
The fickle, restless beloved
    does not want to surrender,
        It does not stay steady and resolute,
Spreading out its colourful wings,
    it flies off to new branches—
With rapt attention you refrain from speech,
    You keep sitting unweariedly on the same seat—
Gradually it will give in,
    The songs will come to an end,
        It will submit to you.

After bewitching her,
    on what lonely path will you take her—
carelessly embracing the unconscious loved one
    in your chariot of darkness !
Where the timeless remains ever a virgin—
    For endless years the touch of light
        draws no line of thrilling delight
            on her body,
where, in the everlasting reserved quarters
    on the other side of creation
        there never enters the slightest footfall
        of the distant stars and planets,
there you will spread out your enormous wings
    without restraint—
Close to your heart
    the newly-wedded bride will tremble,
        newly freed from all bonds.

Gradually will she forget the cosy abode on earth
    strung with grasses and leaves—
        this joyous sunlight, the affection,
            this home, these flowers and leaves ?

Gradually will she lovingly accept you
    as a very close relative and friend—
What speechless conversation there will be
    in the dark bridal chamber !
All the restless pleasures of earth
    will be regarded as mere trifles,
There will be your embodiment-of-love,
    so cordial, solemn, calm,
        and boundless trust,
There will be those fixedly-gazing blue eyes
    that mass of matted hair
        that pervades the whole universe
            and, too, the silent lips—
When the river flows into the ocean,
    will she remember any more
        the various memories of the shore ?

Oh Death, my beloved,
    wait for a while on this earth—
Don't take her now as a bride
    into the realm of the eternal bridal chamber.
She has not yet finished
    all her songs of the dawn, of the evening,
At night she is asleep in the cosy abode
    made pleasant and warm
        by the great heat of her own heart.
She still has to go with the wayfarer-birds
    to the land in the bowers on the seashore
        in search of the joys of fresh springs.
Oh Death, why have you come just now ?
    Why have you sat down in her cosy abode ?
Do you want to darken all her love
    by loving her ?

If it's really a momentary game
    on this earth of clay—
all these meetings face-to-face,
    all those close contacts
        are nought but ephemeral fairs;

If do or die love is a mere bond of falsehood,
    if, at a touch, it falls loose
        and then there is lamenting for a while,
    then only you are permanent,
        only you are endless,
            only you are the final destiny,
    then all desires, all loves
        get their final rest in your darkness—
So then, Oh Death, go away at once,
    Don't break up this play-house now,
        Wait a little,
            Don't steal away my few days.

At some time evening will come,
    In the far-off temple the conch shell will sound,
        calling all to the arati of lights,
The birds will be silent,
    Crickets will chirp in the deep forest,
All my work will come to an end,
    All the victories and defeats
        sustained in the battle of the world
            will be over,
Sound sleep will fall on the eyes
    of the oh-so-weary wayfarer,
The last light of evening will disappear
    over the horizon,
        Darkness will cover the earth,
In the distance,
    only on the endless path of the journey,
        the lamp of stars will be burning.
There will come down on the eyes of those
    who, after sleep, are sitting on their beds
        and staring ahead blankly in the dim light,
            the burden of tiredness like one
                that follows a sleepless night—
One by one all the intimate companions,
    men and women, will go to their own homes,

Gradually, at midnight
    the empty lamp will go out by itself,
A swelling breeze
    will bring the fragrance of unseen flowers,
The sound of waves from an unknown shore
    will come and fill the darkness completely—
Oh Death, at that auspicious moment
    come as a bridegroom to the side of the
                            lonely bed.
My beloved will spread out her tired arms
    and will lovingly hold your hands,
Then recite a mantra and take her,
    Make her blood red lips pale
        from the intensity of your kiss.

CREATIONS OF MY MIND

(Poetry; Beauty,
    the creeper of my imagination,
        the wealth of my life-long intense efforts)

O dearly beloved,
    there will be no work today—
I'm putting aside all compositions, books, songs.
    Just this once come and sit at my side.
Just for today there will be whispering
    and lilting songs between you and me,
just enjoying silently the golden wine
    of this evening's sun's rays
until the veins and veinlets of my heart
    fill with the flow of grace and charm,
until the bondage of painful feelings
    breaks out into great delight,
until I forget all—
    all the unsatisfied longings of my heart,
        all the sounds of music that became silent,

all the nectar of pleasure that disappeared
    without satisfying my desires
        after coming to the tip of my lips.
May this peace, this pleasure
    bring to my life's pain, affliction, insatiety
        a placid and dim charm,
            a compassionate, soft glow,
                deep and beautiful.

Oh Beauty of my imagination,
    put aside the beena and come !
Cling to me, embrace me with your empty hands,
    fill your arms with embraces—
With the touch of your arms, like lotus stalks,
    a thrill rises in heart-felt delight,
        my restless heart trembles,
            my eyes fill with tears,
                my enchanted body is deeply moved.
My heart just shines
    to the tips of my extremities
as if the bonds of my sense organs,
    are about to break at any moment.
Spread out half of your anchal,
    Let me sit at your side.
Call me in most endearing tones,
    call me 'dear', call me 'dearest'.
Set your face covered with dishevelled tresses
    on my breast and in a soft voice
        whisper secretly to my heart
            anything you wish, anything meaningless
                but full of emotion.
Oh dearest, when I ask you for a kiss,
    don't smile slightly, bending your head
        and moving your face away.
Into the cup of my lips pour happiness,
    bright red and full of nectar.
Bestow on your devoted bee a full-mouthed kiss
    and heaps of smiles, loving and gracious.

Like a newly blooming flower incline
    the matchless stalk of your neck
        and lift your face toward me,
Place the deep shade of your two large eye lids
    over my face in calm trust, full confidence.
If tears come to your eyes,
    we'll weep together.
If a soft smile drifts
    to your charming cheeks, then, sitting
        on my lap, embrace me, put your face
            on my shoulder, smile with half-shut eyes.
If any words come to mind, for half the night
    murmur them sweetly with softened pleasure
        like a fountain—innumerable tales,
            memories, waves of imagination—
                in your low, honeyed, lilting voice,
            If you like songs, then sing.
O my beloved, engrossed as your heart is,
    if you just want to sit silent, still, calm,
        only staring in front of you,
            then I'll remain that way too.
I'll gaze at the nearby 'Padma'
    lying in the evening light under the high bank,
        extending her body on the spread-out anchal
        like a woman tired and beautiful.
On the eyes falls darkness
    like the lids of the eyes.
The evening star rises slowly and cautiously
    on top of the forest beside the river bank,
The night makes a bed for her,
    spreading out darkness in the endless world.
Both of us will gaze at the boundless darkness,
    There is nothing else anywhere,
        There are only we two creatures
            close to each other in endless solitude,
                There is only your hand held by mine.
Doleful separations
    eclipse the whole of creation—

Only one side is bent on destruction,
    The rest is a timorous union, two hands,
        two hearts trembling like tremulous pigeons.
In both their hearts there blooms
    a single fear, a single hope,
        a single tearful, meek love.

The night will pass in this way,
    in indolent pleasure.
Oh unassuming one, O first love of my life,
    O moon of beauty in the sky of my destiny !
Do you remember the day in my early childhood
    when we met half-known, half unknown
        in a certain grove of blooming jasmine ?
You are the daughter
    of this earth's neighbour.
O companion, how you controlled and lead
    at pleasure a restless boy of this world !
You used to come in the fresh dawn at sleep's end
    as a young girl, wearing a white robe,
recently bathed in a stream of dawn rays,
    your cheerful face like a blooming flower.
You used to take me to the grove
    to gather shephali blossoms.
Again and again you bewitched me,
    making me neglect my childhood duties;
        throwing away my books,
            snatching away my chalk,
                showing me secret paths, you freed me
                      from the prison of the classroom.
Somewhere in my room you used to take me
    into solitude in a mysterious mansion.
How you used to play on the empty roof
    of my room under the sky !
With what amazing words you enchanted me,
    delightful as dreams, meaningless;
        Only you know if they were true or false.

Pearls were swinging from your ears,
    Golden bangles graced your arms,
Stray ringlets played upon your cheeks,
    Light sparkled in your clear eyes
        like divergent rays in a pure stream.
Even before we knew each other well
    we played and romped about together,
        carefree, trusting.
Our chatting, like our clothes,
    was scattered about, mislaid.

Then, one day, I don't remember when,
    in the grove of my life, in the springtime of youth,
        the first southern breeze sighed.
Hundreds of desires and hopes blossomed out,
    Then, suddenly startled by my own songs,
        I was amazed as I saw:
You, the goddess of my heart and imagination,
    had come, at some time, within me.
In your own inner room
    you were sitting proudly as a queen.
Who had welcomed you ?
    Who received you at the door with shouts of joy ?
Who had filled their anchals with fresh flowers
    and showered your lowered head
        joyfully, lovingly ?
What a delightful ceremony took place
    in my world to the charming tune of the flute
        in the beautiful mode of shahana
when, as a blushing bride in a crimson sari,
    you went up the path covered with blooming
                              flowers
    and entered the room of my heart
        forever—
there, in His secret abode,
    where God remains awake, attentive
        to my joys and sorrows,

where all my shame, my hopes and fears
 are ever a tremble, so tender to the touch !
You were my playmate,
 Now you have become the mistress
  of my heart of hearts,
   the goddess, the mistress of my life
Where are those tears of joy ?
 That restless agitation is gone,
  That was a part of childhood.
The loving look is as grave
 as the clear blue sky.
The tranquil smile is bedewed with tears,
 Your full body is like a blooming vine,
Love and affection are jingling
 in the solemn song
  arising from the golden threads
   of your beena in endless sorrow.
Since then O Beloved, I've been at a loss:
 My wanting you is boundless.
On what bank of the world is your homeland ?
 How far will your songs take me ?
On what dream world will you imprison me
 with the thrill of your songs,
  like a bewildered deer ?
Is there any language to express this pain ?
 Is there any satisfying of these desires ?
Is there any shore to this vast sea
 on which you, as helmsman, have set afloat
  your beautiful boat ?
All around and day and night
 are the indistinct roaring waves
  expressing something I can't understand.
The boat of my mind runs before the breeze of pain
 on the ocean of beauty.
So often I fear
 that the sail of my heart-boat will tear.
I feel confident when I behold your large eyes
 fully assuring and heartening with promise,

Immense trust awakes in my heart
    that there is an extensive beach
        somewhere at the edge of this beauty;
            Our dwelling is on the shore of desires.
O honeyed mystery !
    you are smiling softly
        while looking into my face.
O love-smitten,
    what do you want to say to me ?
My spouse,
    what do you want to explain to me ?
Words won't achieve anything,
    Just cover my whole body, my heart
        with your anchal.
By force take my whole being,
    O take everything.
O beloved, I want to hear the mystery of your heart,
    placing my naked breast against yours.
Like fingers, the throbbing of your heart
    will pluck the strings of my heart.
The sound of song waves will murmur,
    and, quivering, will pervade my whole life.
It doesn't matter whether I understand,
    whether I say anything, whether I compose
        any songs, whether I go up the path
            of poetry attracting my shy heart !
Only I would forget, ignore the lyrics
    and tremble, full of songs.
Like a star
    I would only burn with delight
        in a quivering flame.
Like a wave
    I would only break against your wave.
I would only live or die,
    I would do nothing more.
Give me that vast stream
    by which, all at once, I can fill my life
        silently, furiously, recklessly.

Oh Fancied Beauty, Oh Dweller in my longings !
    Oh Light-clothed, Oh Silent speaking,
Oh Flawless Beauty, in your rebirth
    will you become incarnate
        in some earthly home ?
Now you are adrift in boundlessness,
    You are frolicking from heaven to earth,
You are dyeing your anchal in sunset gold,
    You are making your ornamental girdle
        with the melted gold of sunrise.
Now you are spreading your charming full youth
    on the brimming river,
Now you are expressing your restless,
    longing-pain in the scented breath
        of the spring breeze.
Now in the sleeping full moon night
    you are alone, and, with tired hands,
        you are spreading out your milk-white
        bed-of-separation
            across the empty sky.
Now, during this early autumn morning
    you are gathering shefali blossoms;
In the end you forget to string a garland,
    You throw it all at the foot of a tree.
With your hair unbound, in a fit of indifference
    you sit in the shade of a deep forest.
In the afternoon, in the shade of a bakul tree
    you are, with tremulous fingers,
        weaving cloth with the sparkling light
        and shade.
No one knows in what densely leafy grove
    on the bank of what lake, you are,
        in the exhausted daylight, singing
            a multan tune in the plaintive voice
        of a dove.
No one knows when, coming secretly,
    you touch and harry my heart amusedly.

Laughing in a fickle, sweet voice,
    you flee quickly
        if I try to catch hold of your anchal.
You mock me, you taunt me
    and quickly vanish in the blue of the sky—
        all this after having aroused
            endless desires in my heart.
When I am immersed in my work, suddenly startled,
    your loose-robed dazzling beauty
        flashes naked lightning and disappears.
When, in the dark twilight, I sit alone
    beside the window, and, covering my face
        with my hands I weep for the light
            of affection like a motherless child—
I wish that the stream of night darkness
    would wipe out from the canvas of creation
        the marks of my feeble and meaningless
            existence—
then, O Compassionate One, you show yourself,
coming silently from the the end of the calm night
    blazing with the light of the stars.
With your anchal you wipe away my tears,
    You look into my face with eyes
        loving, inquiring, compassionate.
You kiss my eyes,
    You brush your cool hands across my forehead,
I don't know when you go away with silent tread,
    without saying anything, after filling
        your poet's heart with comfort
            and lulling him to sleep.
Would that 'you' in human form surrender
    to me, give itself to me ?
Would you touch the earth
    with your crimson feet ?
Would you take a charming, pleasing form
    at the edge of the universe
        as you remove your own all pervading self,

from all places—from inside and outside,
   from the universe, from the sky,
      from land and water ?
Would you take your movement from the river,
   from vines ? Would you spread it out in waves
      throughout your whole body in different
         ways of dancing, bending your arms,
            inclining your neck,
               displaying vast emotions ?
Oh Beauty, what blue skirt would you wear ?
   What kind of bracelets would you wear ?
How would you put up your hair,
   braiding it with care and skill ?
How your soft hair falling on your neck
   would quiver like rain-tree blossoms
      fanned by the breeze !
I don't know how the sight of Sraban's
   thick, cool clouds—blue, charming, soft—
      would look in a woman's eyes !
How that sight would bring a night of joy
   to the enchanted heart,
      to the continuous deep shade of the lids,
         to the lustre of deep darkness !
How the lips would be eagerly expectant
   to bestow nectar !
How they would be silent, speechless
   yet full of expression !
How the body would blossom out in youthfulness
   and display tiers of grace and charm
      welling up in incessant, unbearable beauty !
I know, I know, my intimate Friend,
   if we meet again face to face
      on the path of rebirth,
   I would halt suddenly, taken aback.
Trembling, the slumbering past would be startled
   and regain awareness,
I know I would remember those black eyes,

known for ever, as the pole star of my whole life.
Taking light from my eyes,
    taking desires from my heart,
        my secret love created this face.
Deep in your heart, would you know me?
    Would there be love and union between us?
Young Lady, would you ever give me a garland
    strung with the flowers of spring?
O Mistress of my heart,
    would I ever bind you in a tight embrace
        to my heart's content?
Exchanging touches, embraces,
    would we die at the doors of our bodies
        in delightful enchantment?
Every day of my life would get your light
    without intermission.
Each night of my life would be splendid
    with your charming beauty;
        Would the tunes of your songs resound
            throughout my body and my heart?
Your bright smile would remain
    in all the pleasures of my life;
Your tears would fall
    on all the pains of my life.
In every bit of my work
    there would be your helping hands,
You would always enkindle gracious light
    in my abode,
Are these all only the fruitless dreams of desire,
    the deceptions of imaginings?
Who has such divine knowledge,
    who can give me certain proof—
As a woman, were you or were you not
    blossoming in beauty in the forest of my life
        in a previous existence,
            unfolding in love?
Beloved, at the time of union
    you were bound to one place only;

During separation you broke the bond
    and today are universal
        for you pervade everything—
            Everywhere I look, I see you.
The incense has burnt out,
    its scented smoke fills everything.
You were the mistress of my home,
    Shattering this abode, you appeared
        in the poetry of the world—
Then, by what sort of enchantment, Eternally,
                      Beloved,
    did you give yourself to my heart,
then how did you awake in me various tunes,
    abounding remembrances (of the past) ?
That is why I still entertain the hope
    of embracing you one day.
That is the way the whole world
    is lighting and extinguishing,
        creating and destroying
           like the light of the firefly,
                sometimes imaginary. sometimes real.

The night is far advanced,
    The lamp is about to go out;
I don't know when the last golden streak of evening
    disappeared in the western sky
        on the far-off shore of the Padma (River).
The Great Bear has risen in the black sky,
    The young wife has filled her last pitcher
        and has gone back home,
I see the night, the dark fortnight,
    the long path, the empty field,
        the wayfarer from elsewhere getting shelter
           in the home of some householder;
Some time back there died down the hubbub
    from the village at the side of the field;
I don't know when the evening lamp was lit
    or when it went out in the silent, broken-down

peasant's house at the riverside—
I don't know anything.

Oh Beloved, I don't know what I've been saying;
Half-consciously it entered my heart, dream-like.
Oh Dearest, did anyone overhear me?
Did you understand what I've been saying?
Is there any meaning to it all?
I've forgotten all I said;
It's only that on the shore of this sleepy night
the endless ocean of the tears of my heart
has welled up in sombre tones.

Oh Sleep, Oh Peace, Oh Beloved,
spellbound, silent, doleful Beauty,
take me to your bosom—
Lay me down carefully on the bed of oblivion,
death cool, white.

NOT APPRECIATED

Early in the morning the fresh sun was bringing
articles of the dawn's worship
on a platter of gold.
The shoreless blue water was rippling softly,
A crimson line was shining
on the garland of sunshine.
Then the sun rose
to the forehead of the sky.
Sitting on the shore,
I was weaving a net.
Calmly and leisurely
I once looked into the deep water—
I heard someone's message pulling at my heart,
Carefully I raised the net over my head,
turned around
and threw it far into the water.

I don't know how many things
   were caught in the net.
One gives off rays like a smile,
   One pours out cruel tears
     and is on the verge of falling,
Another one is like the show of shyness
   on the cheeks of a bride—
     that day at dawn on the shore of the sea.

Morning has gone by,
   The sun, having left the east,
     proudly rises to the top of the sky.
Forgetting hunger and thirst,
   I cast the net and pull it in again.
Then the dust of twilight rose into the air,
   into the gray sky,
Lowing happily,
   the cows hurried to their shelters.

By the time I returned home extremely tired
   with the burden of the day,
     the moon had risen in the sky,
There was no one on the village path,
   Deep shadows covered the earth,
My eyes close with dreams—
   A separated bird is calling in a plaintive tone.

After finishing her housework,
   she was sitting in the garden
     and wearing a garland.
A few blossoms fell loose from a tree,
   She tears the flowers into shreds,
     whiling away the time absent-mindedly.

Once I move toward her, once I draw back;
   I go up close to her with my eyes cast down.
I place all that I have at her feet,
   covering them;

Looking them over, she said,
   'I don't know any of these thing.'
When I heard this,
   I stood there with my head bowed.

I thought to myself:
   Oh how I have wasted the whole day
      in child's play !
I don't know by what enchantment
   I went to the shore of the shoreless sea,
      I plunged in out of curiosity—
From the unknown sea I brought up
   a large number of unknown lumps of earth.

I never fight,
   I'm not curious about what is in the market
                                            place—
Was I right in offering such wealth
   that is attained without any effort !
One who has no sorrow,
   one who has no longing for thirst—
      what will she do with these !
         I gathered them up, quite embarrassed.

All night long I sat by the door,
   one by one I threw them all away
      at the end of the path.
I went away indifferent—
   without wealth, without happiness—
The next day at dawn a wayfarer picked them all up
   and went to his own land.

BY RIVER

The sky is overcast with deep clouds,
   The wind is blowing at full speed,
Thunder clatters every now and then,
    Waves rise up on the river,
      The wind is blowing at full speed.

Rows of trees are swaying on the shore
   with restless rustling,
Lightning flashes everywhere,
   piercing the darkness,
     Rows of trees are swaying on the shore.

Rain is pouring down
   in incessant streams,
It stops for a while,
   then, like a madman,
     it bursts out with double delight,
       Rain is pouring down in incessant streams.

Because of the clouds
   all signs of paths have disappeared,
     so time stands still.
When I look at the sky,
   I can't tell whether the day has passed,
     So time stands still.

I have tied up my boat at the shore,
   I remain there all day long.
Even now a long trip
   lies ahead of me.
Dark night is coming on,
   I have tied up my boat at the shore.
Sitting alone in a corner of the boat,
   I muse—
After spreading her bedding on the floor,
   she is passing the night without sleep,

Her eyes are sleepless.
I muse while I sit.

She trembles
  when she hears the rumbling of the clouds.
    She presses her hands against her bosom.
Staring at the sky,
  she sees no reason to be confident.
She passes the whole night in alarm
  as she keeps hearing
    the rumbling of the clouds.

Sometimes the door bangs
  from the blowing of the wind.
The lamp is about to go out,
  Shadows are trembling in fright,
Tears flow from her eyes,
  Her heart quivers violently.

Repeatedly her startled eyes come to mind,
  There is a fierce storm outside,
Thunder claps rip the sky,
  The sky is wailing.
    Her eyes come to mind.

The sky is overcast with dense clouds,
  The wind is blowing wildly,
Thunder-bolts rumble now and then,
  Waves dance on the river.
    The wind is blowing wildly.

TEMPLE

I made a temple
  at the cost of great suffering
    and over a long period of time.
I did not make any door or window,
  There's darkness everywhere;
Carefully carrying loads of stones from a hill,
  I made a temple.

Setting up the deity inside,
  I remained gazing at her face.
Throwing out this threefold world
  and forgetting all the people in the world,
    I meditated on the deity with rapt attention.
      setting up the deity inside.

I spent endless nights
  lighting hundreds of scented lamps.
From the bejewelled gold cup
  the smoke of scented incense rose.
The heavy scent of fragrant wood
  escaped into the air,
    My heart was overwhelmed.
    I spent endless nights.

Sleepless and in rapt attention
  I drew oh so many pictures on all the walls.
They were all so wonderful,
  not modelled anything that existed before—
    in oh so many colours,
      in oh so many forms !
No one can describe them—
  all the pictures I Drew on the walls.

Snake-maidens raised their hoods
  and wound themselves round the pillars
    in hundreds of twists.

Swarming all over the top
  were grotesque monsters, on their heads
    holding up the burden of the stone roof.
      Snake-maidens raised their hoods.

There were on so many outside-of-creation designs,
  Innumerable kings of birds were flying about,
Among the creepers, like flowers,
  there bloomed the faces of women,
    showing their beauty, lowering their gaze
      amorously, demurely, coyly.
        There were
          oh so many outside-of-creation designs.

In this world full of sounds
  only this temple had no sound.
I sat on a tiger skin
  and composed various kinds of rhythms.
I recited mantras day and night
  in a humming tune
    in the soundless temple.

Oh so many days went by in this way
  I knew nothing else.
    I was so engrossed in myself.
My heart was as steadfast as an upturned flame,
  Weakened by the heat of emotion,
    I fell into a swoon.
      Oh so many days went by in this way.

With a frightful bang
  thunder once crashed inside my temple.
Intense pain seared my heart,
  cutting it like a fiery serpent.
    Thunder crashed inside my temple.

Suddenly the stone structure fell apart,
  Day appeared in my temple.

Breaking up my silent meditation
  and removing all the serious obstacles,
    the endless tunes of ordinary life
      came pouring in.
        Suddenly the stone structure fell apart.

Once I looked at the deity,
  Light fell on her face.
On Her forehead new sings of majesty shone,
  A smile of full favour appeared on Her lips.
    Once I looked at the deity.

The lamp was getting dim in shame,
  It wanted to hide in perpetual darkness.
All the pictures drawn on the walls
  were bound with chains like dreams,
They were stricken with shame
  but could not escape.
    The lamp was getting dim in shame.
The songs which I had failed to compose
  now burst forth in all directions,
The sun lit my lamp,
  Nature herself drew my pictures.
    Hundreds of poets composed oh so many songs
      in various rhythms.
        Oh what songs burst out today
          in all directions !

All the doors of my temple have opened up—
  There is accord between what is interior
    and what is exterior (to me).
My deity awoke
  at the touch of God.
The imprisoned night fled
  on the wings of darkness.
    All the doors of my temple have opened up.

UNIVERSAL DANCE

Who will play the music
   in very deep, pleasant, sonorous tones !
The heart will dance
   and will forget itself,
     Bonds will break,
       There will be great delight.
There will be new rhythms in new songs,
   The full moon will awake new desires
     in the sea of the heart.

Frequent tearful smiles will light up her face,
   The glowing rays of the morning sun
     will blossom out in her eyes.
He holds the instrument in His right hand,
   Then the jingling golden strings quiver
     as they waft charming hymns
       into the clear blue sky.

In a wailing, welling, restless, all-pervading
   sweet murmur, all will come out swiftly
     from all sides in a mad stream.
They will all surge forward in a massive billow,
   surrounding Him (who plays the music)
     with great delight
       as they cross over obstacles, dancing
         and trampling on the thorns on the path.

Thirsting for heaven
   that sea of mankind will destroy the chains
     of bondage,
With boundless delight
   they will hold the whole world in their laps.
Sunbeams sporting on the waves
   will scatter golden rays.
Obstacles and dangers, sadness and death
   will drift away like foam.

Oh ! It seems I can hear someone,
   sitting in the sky and eternally playing
      in appealing, grave and sonorous tones
         that are full of deep mystery.
The planetary world becomes frenzied,
   They go dancing and become restless forever.
      Their anchals of lustre
         fall loose now and then.

Oh ! Nobody knows what a great tune this is.
   Nobody knows who is playing, who is listening.
Swinging and swelling, the ocean is dancing
   like a many-headed snake.
The dense forest is swaying in joy,
   raising hundreds of arms to the endless sky,
      forgetting the lyrics
         while intent on singing,
            rustling day and night.

The spring gushes out on the stony path,
   overflowing with delight,
      She moves rhythmically and beautifully
         to steal away the heart of the stone.
From her sweet voice there arises constantly
   a babbling tune, soft and pleasing.
      The jewelled anklets on her moving feet
         are ever jingling.

The six seasons are dancing ceaselessly
   arm-to-arm, wearing new robes
      of various colours, such as green and gold.
With their every motion
   oh so many wild flowers are blooming
      and falling off, overwhelmed.
The massive heart of the earth
   gets filled with laughter and weeping.

The beasts and birds, the worms and insects
  and all the streams of life are bustling about.
The waves (of these streams) are breaking
  on the shore of death in some great play.
Somewhere there is light,
  Somewhere there is shade,
New lives are waking up.
  The wonderful material world, full of sensation,
    is effervescing like so many bubbles.

Listen ! Someone is playing day and night,
  while sitting in the heart,
    wonderful music on the instrument of time—
Some people hear it, some do not.
I cannot understand its meaning.
  Many virtuous, talented and wise people
    are thinking about it.
The great purposes of mankind
  constantly rise and fall
    according to its sway.

Why is there no joy only here ?
  I don't see any stars in the western sky,
    I see no dawn in the east.
Everywhere there are only stone walls,
  like a worldwide graveyard,
    devouring, eclipsing, stifling
      innumerable lives
        in unmoved pride.

The stream of earthly life
  flows out a great distance like the Ganges.
The stream (of the unearthly world) only dries up
  like a desert, barren and sand-gray.
It has no movement, no song,
  It has no work, no life,
It is like total extinction,
  wearing a crown of darkness.

My heart weeps
  when it mingles with human hearts,
    when it has to move along
      with the whole world on the great highway.
During the whole of my life I have been
  like a dead person,
    overcome by insensibility.
Who will give this thirsting heart
  a drop of the nectar of life ?

Who will inspire these people to dance
  to the sound of that music
    which excites the world !
Who will revive them
  by inspiring them to drink
    the life of the universe !
Who will tear off the fetters of racism !
  The wind will blow into the open heart;
    Who will break up this decayed cage
      of baseless fright !

Let the music of the world play
  in very deep, pleasing, grave and sonorous tones.
Let the heart dance in self-oblivion !
  Let the bonds break !
    Let great delight awake !
Let new rhythms arise in new songs !
  Let the full moon arouse new desires
    in the sea of the heart !

HARD TO KNOW

Can't you understand me ?
  Calmly and sadly your eyes are inquiring about me,
    trying to figure me out
      just as the moon looks at the ocean
        with motionless face turned downward.

I have not kept anything concealed from you.
   Whatever there is in me is all open to you,
      my wide open, unveiled heart.
I have shown you everything,
   so that you can comprehend me—
      Still you can't understand me ?

If this love was only a gem
   I would break it up into hundreds of pieces,
Carefully I'd consider their various shapes
   and sizes one by one,
Then, stringing them into a necklace,
   I'd put it around your neck.

If it was only a flower,
   perfectly round, beautiful, small,
      about to blossom at dawn,
         swinging in the spring breeze,
I'd pluck it carefully from the stalk
   and put it on your black hair.

Beloved, here is my whole heart.
   Where is the water, where is the shore,
      Its limits are not known,
         It's the home of endless mystery.
Oh my queen,
   you don't know the beginning or the end,
      yet it is your capital.

I don't know what I want to make you understand.
   I don't know what is playing deep in my heart
      in a silent song day and night—
         pervading the sky with soundless calm
            just like the sound of night.

If it was only happiness,
   then only a single smile

coming to the tip of the lips
would awake joy.
In a moment you would understand
the message of my heart,
I would not have to say anything.

If it was only sorrow,
then seeing two drops of tears filling the eyes,
the sad lips, the pale face—
you would perceive directly the pain in my
heart,
Words would tell you silently.

O my beloved, it is only the love of my heart—
whose happiness, sadness and pain
have no beginning, no ending—
ever distressed, ever filled with gold,
ever-new eagerness awakes day and night,
so I can't make you understand me.

It doesn't matter
if you don't understand me !
You will always see me in new lights
and study me day and night.
One can understand half of love,
a half of the heart—
Who can understand the whole ?

SWINGING

Tonight I'll play the game of death with my life.
It's a cloudy rainy season day
and the sky is ink dark.
Look ! All around the torrent of rain is weeping.
I have set adrift my raft
in the fearful struggle
on the waves of earthly life.

I have come out at night,
   disdaining the dreams of sleep.

Oh ! Today what great delight there is
   in the storm, in the sky, in the ocean !
      Swing it ! Make it swing !
The frenzied storm comes laughing loudly
   from behind and gives a push,
It seems as if this is the uproar
   of countless ghost children.
      Swing it ! Make it swing !
In the sky, in the netherworld,
   among the insane, among the frenzied
      there is a confused hullabaloo.
         Swing it ! Make it swing !

Today my life awakes and sits near my heart.
   Now and then it quivers
      as it tightly clasps my heart.
My heart dances in delight
   with the pleasure of a cruel and close embrace.
Near my heart my life is perturbed
   with fear, with great delight.

With immense love I kissed her eyelids;
   Keeping my head beside hers,
      I called her oh so many loving names
         in tones soft and tender.
On moonlit nights
   I sang to her in gunjar strains.
With immense love and with both hands
   I gave her all that I had
      that was pleasant and delightful.

At last
   my life became weary, on the bed of pleasure,
      with the charm of indolence.
      with the obsession of love.

No more does she awake at my touch,
  The garland of flowers seems a heavy burden.
Day and night she passes in drowsiness;
  Painless, feelingless aversion
    enters my heart
      with the obsession of love.

Perhaps, by pouring out pleasure after pleasure,
  I have lost my sweet love;
    I cannot find her when I seek her.
The lamp in the bridal chamber
  is about to go out.
Anxiously I look about ;
  Only heaps of withered flowers are piled up.
Sinking into the unfathomable ocean of dreams,
  I struggle to find someone.

Alas ! Upto now
  I have carefully kept her on my bed.
Lest she suffer any pain,
  lest she suffer sadness,
day and night I most tenderly decorated the bed
  of the bridal chamber with banks of flowers.
Locking the door of my secret chamber
  I have guarded her with great care.

That is why
  I think I have to play a new game tonight.
Holding on to the ropes,
  we'll sit very close together
    on the swing of death.
The storm will come and give it a shove
  while laughing uproariously—
Tonight I'll play the game-of-swinging
  with my life.

Swing it ! Make it swing !
  Raise a violent storm on this great ocean.

Again I have my loved one,
  My heart is thoroughly satisfied.
The suppressed cry of extinction
  awoke my beloved.
What great waves of delight rise up
  in the blood of my heart !
What great joy awakes inside and outside
  of my heart !
The hair is flaring out,
  The anchal is flapping.
The garland of wild flowers
  is stirred up by the excited wind.
Feverishly the bangles are clinking,
  The anklet bells are jingling.
    Swing it ! Make it swing !

Come, oh storm !
  Snatch the veils off my loved one !
    Take off her veil !
      Swing it ! Make it swing !
Today I have to come face to face with my life,
  We'll get to know each other,
    casting aside all fear, all shame.
My heart will touch your heart,
  We'll be filled with emotion,
    Swing it ! Make it swing !
Smashing to bits the dream, the myth,
  today we two mad ones
    have come into the open.
      Swing it ! Make it swing !

(Sorry ! Verse 4 starts with:
  Alas ! Upto now I have carefully......)

HEART-JAMUNA

Oh Beloved, if you want to fill your pitcher,
   come, come to the stream of my heart.
The swirling deep water will weep
   as it washes around your tender feet.
Today the heavy rain is at its thickest,
   Both shores of my heart are overcast with clouds
     like thick hair.
Why, I know that jingling sound of your ankle bells;
   Who are you, coming alone and oh so slowly ?
Oh Beloved, if you want to fill your pitcher,
   come, come to the stream of my heart.

If you just want to remain sitting absent-mindedly,
   (after setting adrift your pitcher,)
     why, here the grass is green,
       here the sky is fresh blue,
   the forest is blooming with full blown flowers.
Your mind will wander out of itself
   through those dark eyes of yours,
     Your anchal will get loose and fall off.
Oh what things will come to mind
   while you're sitting on the grass
     in the asoka arbour on the green shore !
If you just want to remain sitting absent-mindedly
   after setting afloat your pitcher......

If you want to bathe, then come down here
   where the water is deep.
What's the use of wearing that short blue skirt ?
   Leave it on the shore today,
     The blue stream will robe your shyness,
Waves of love and affection will take hold of
                             your body,
   They will flow over your breast,
     over your neck—
Swirling all around, sometimes they weep,

sometimes they laugh in various ways,
   washing against you softly, sweetly.
If you want to bathe, then come, come down here
   where the water is deep.

If you want to die, then come,
   come and plunge into the stream.
Like death, the blue stream is a thing of beauty,
   ever bottomless, ever shoreless,
     cool, refreshing, calm and deep.
There is no day, no night—
   no beginning, no end, no sort of measure,
     In those depths no music plays at all.
Forget, forget everything,
   Free yourself of all bonds,
Leave behind all work, all activity,
   In all you do: come to the shore.
If you want to die, then come,
   come and plunge into the stream.

PASSING YOUTH

The night that is passing away today—
   how can I bring her back?
     Why are my eyes futilely shedding tears?
Oh intimate friend,
   take these robes, take these ornaments,
     This flower garland has become unbearable—
What a night I have passed
   on the bed-of-separation.
The night that is passing away today—
   how can I bring her back?

In vain have I come to this trysting place
   on the bank of the Jamuna.
So intensely have I loved,
   bearing in vain my heart's desire.

Now at last, at the end of night
  I'm returning to my unhappy abode—
    with a glum face, with tired steps,
      with a listless mind.
Alas ! The night that is passing away—
  how can I bring her back ?

How often the moon rose in the sky
  in the deep of night !
In the forest the flowers danced in the breeze,
  agitated by the fragrance.
The sweet notes of the river,
  the rustling whisper of the trees
    seemed to me like a dream.
From the distance came songs
  that reached my hearing.
The night that is passing away today—
  how can I bring her back ?

I felt as if she had called me,
  as if she always remembered me.
She would always bring me perfect love.
  She would make the stream of my youth wakeful.
Coming at midnight,
  she would bind me with bonds of affection.
Alas ! The night that is passing away—
  how can I bring her back ?

Oh ! Then it's better to forget,
  What's the use of more weeping ?
I have to go on,
  Then why oh why does my heart keep looking
                            back ?
How long will I stay sitting like a fool,
  day and night at the gate of the bower ?
    Now spring is over in my life.
Alas ! The night that has passed away—
  how can I ever get her back ?

FULL AUGUST

The river is brimming to the shore,
  The fields are full of paddy.
I'm pondering—
  What song will I sing ?
Screwpine flowers are blooming
  in the underbrush near the riverside.
The bakul grove is calm
  with its burden of flowers.
    My heart is full to the brim.

Sparkling are the leaves,
  Glittering is the light;
Thinking, thinking am I about her,
  the one with the black eyes.
There are rows and rows of kadam
  with their beautiful leaves,
Darkness gets filled with flower fragrance
  and becomes deeper dark still.
To whom shall I tell this ?

The day is cheerful and radiant,
  The rains have come to an end.
I'm wondering what I'll give (her)
  as a gift today.
Cloudlets in tiers are roaming about,
  wafted around by a spiritless wind,
    as if they were dejected.
I'd like to break myself
  into a hundred pieces.

It seem as if the day has become paralysed
  through indolence.
I wonder
  what the other one is thinking.
There are lots of kamini flowers on the branches,
  there without any effort.

From time to time throughout the day
  they become loose and fall to the ground.
How the flute plays
  all morning, all evening.

The forest is filled
  with the merry songs of the birds.
I wonder
  why tears come to my eyes.
A doyel, swinging on a branch,
  is singing an ambrosial song.
    A pair of doves stay hidden in the leaves.
The sum of all this
  quite overwhelms me.

REPROACH

Don't look at me so miserably.
  Don't sing in such a sweet doleful voice.
In the morning during all your work
  don't go walking back and forth
    through my courtyard.
      Don't look at me so miserably.
Carefully I've kept my secrets in my heart,
  Vainly you wander, begging for that gem.
It's a trifle, it's nothing—
  It's just a pain,
    blood-red, with a few tears.
      Don't look at me so miserbly.

With what expectation
  are you knocking at my door ?
    I don't know what you think about me !
I'm here to hide my shame, my shyness,
  I have no queenly attire,
    wearing today worn-out rags,

my desires.
   Don't look at me so miserably.

Oh what wealth you have brought me
  with two full hands.
Don't go away,
  throwing it all in the dust.
If I want to pay off this debt,
  what is there to do it with,
    Where can I find it ?
I'd have to sell myself all life long.
  Don't look at me so miserably.

I thought to myself:
  I'll remain in a corner of my room,
I'll put up with my secret sorrow
  in my own heart.
Why should I hope—
  There are no expressions
    for what I want to say;
The longing, the desire is there,
  I don't know how to attain my goal.
    Don't look at me so miserably.

Can I ever sing all with the tune
  with which you have filled your flute ?
When I start to sing,
  the song breaks off,
    I can't stop the foolish tears.
      Don't look at me so miserably.

You have come, wearing a garland,
  in new attire, in lovely adornment.
Here
  where is a golden platter,
    where are flowers,
      where is a garland—

who will carefully decorate the bridal chamber ?
  Don't look at me so miserably.

Oh intimate friend.
  you have strayed from the path
    and have come into this room.
Who exchanges garlands in the dark !
  From nightfall I've been lying alone
    on the hard ground,
      passing the night-of life
        extinguishing the lamp !
          Don't look at me so miserably.

SHYNESS

I have given all of my heart, all of my life
  but not my shyness.
After looking at myself,
  I've had to cover myself day and night
    carefully, cautiously.

This transparent robe, Oh beloved,
  is mocking me,
    I can't keep hold of it all the time.
      You cast a side glance my way
        and laugh inwardly,
          so I'm completely mortified with shame.

I don't notice when my anchal flies loose
  in the southern breeze.
My heart, overwhelmed with delight,
  blossoms out in my body,
    Then awareness returns in an instant.

I live in a suffocating room
  and, when I feel like choking.

>   I loosen the fastening of my garb
>   and sit beside the window,
>   forgetting myself for a while
>   in the pleasant breeze of the evening.

On the buds of my fresh youth
  the light of the full moon falls swooning.
Smiling gently, she lovingly covers my body
  with her overflowing grace and charm.
The breeze is blowing
  against my face, my bosom, my tresses
    in hope of playing.
The fragrance of flowers is drifting
  across the sky.
At such a time you have come,
  I feel it as if in a dream;
    I can't remember anything more.

Let it be, beloved, let it stay,
  Don't take this little bit by force.
    Let me keep this shyness—
      to cover half of myself
        with this bit of shyness
          till the end.

Don't be too hurt to show me your tearful eyes,
  I too have spent many nights weeping.
It seems that I can't explain this to you—
  why, after having given you everything,
    I have tied it all up with shyness—

why I lower my head a little
  and conceal that little bit from you.
No, my friend, it is not a lack of trust,
  It is not a joke or scorn,
    It's not a game of pretending.

Oh beloved, on this spring night
  take this fragrance,
    take this nectar.
      Look at me with love.
Set me swinging on all sides,
  Talk to me in a soft voice,
    Just leave me its tiny stalk.

Supported by that stalk
  I am blossoming out toward you
    in all my loveliness;
Ever new gracefulness
  rolls throughout my body
    in such waves of enchantment—

So it is all day:
  the breeze is playing restlessly,
    spring flowers are blooming on both sides,
Listen, oh beloved, just listen:
  Everything that is mine will be yours,
    Only let me keep this shyness.

PRIZE

That day, when the rain was pouring endlessly,
  the poet's wife said to him,
'You are gathering lots of rhymes
  and only writing a big fat book.
Do you know anything about the roof of this house
  which is about to fall down?
You are making up rhymes long and short—
  These are all trash, having no head or tail,
For these you couldn't get a horse or an elephant,
  You would not even get
    a tiny food grain.
  You have gathered lots of words,

but there's no food in the house.
    What child's play this is !
Abandon Saraswati, the goddess of speech,
    and right now start worshipping Laksmi.
My dear, throw away all your books, all your pens,
    Right now do what you're obliged to do.
You've learnt so much,
    but you haven't learnt how to earn
        the smallest coin.'
At the sight of that wrathful image
    the poet's heart was terror-stricken.
Joking and smiling, he said,
    cupped hands before him supplicatingly,
        'I'm not afraid of your scolding.
            The goddess of wealth is kind to this wretch.
                She is in my home, not in my treasury.
                Who will listen to such talk !
It's my bad luck to have an unfavourable fate.
    Fickle Laksmi is being steady with me
        Bharati, the goddess of speech,
            never stays steady for a moment,
                though I worship her to a great extent.
So I'll be searching for rhymes in heaven and on earth,
    after barring the door.
If I'm heedless even for a moment,
    then all at once everything is ruined.'
Looking serious but smiling to herself,
    the poet's wife said,
'I can't do any more.
    My household work is ruined.
        You only poke fun at it.'
So saying, she made a wry face,
    restlessly jingled her bracelets,
        nervously tugged at her anchal
            and went away with a show of anger.
Seeing her go off swiftly with hurt feelings,
    with her earthly pride suppressed,
        the anxious poet pleaded,

'Don't go in this way, pressing against my heart,
    Even if you don't give in to me,
        I'll take hold of your feet.
Tell me how to do what I have to do.
    I'd like to fill your room with gold and silver—
        Give me the right advice.
If I get even a tiny bit of empty space,
    I'll compress your image into it.
There's no scope for the cultivation
    of the intellect or of talent,
        There's desert everywhere.'

'Oh stop it ! That's enough !
    Don't overdo it,' she said
        with a smile, with a show of anger.
'It's my good luck
    that your love is exactly like your modesty.
There's never a lack of words;
    Whenever I say anything, I get a response.
Oh you nawab-of-words !
    Just once let me see you do
        what I tell you to do
Open the almanac, look for the auspicious momen,
    leave off your idleness for a moment,
        take your books and go to the royal court.
Our king is the champion of the talented
    Oh how many people have grown up and matured !
If you collect verses at home,
    of what value are they ?'
To the poet this was a bolt from the blue:
    He thought, 'I see danger ahead today,
        Never have I known a king or emperor—
            I don't know what fortune
                has in store for me.'
Putting on a smile, he said,
    'Nothing more than this !
        I'll talk about what I have to do—

I can sacrifice my life,
   but I'm afraid that you'll become a widow.
If I have to go,
   then what's the use of delaying ?
Hurry then ! Bring my clothes and ornaments—
   gold earrings, gem-studded coronet,
      my armlet, my golden necklace.
Call my charioteer
   and tell him to bring some good horses.
Arrange for the attendants
   who should go with me.'
The brahminee said,
   'He deserves nothing
      who has no control over his tongue.
If his tongue runs on,
   he has no need of chariot horses.
I've borrowed various items of clothing,
   diamonds, gold and silver
      from the neighbours.
Dress up to your heart's content,
   Just stop that tongue !'
After saying this,
   with swift steps she brought
      various articles of clothing.
His face paling, the poet was thinking,
   'Today things aren't going well.'
The housewife was sitting near him,
   helping him dress, while scrubbing and rubbing.
She herself carefully and tightly
   bound his waistband
She put the turban on his head,
   the necklace on his neck,
      the bracelets on his arms,
         the earrings on his ears.
The more gems she put on him,
   the more the poet looked like a picture.
Even the care of his loving wife
   had to admit defeat.

After several hours spent this way,
   she finished dressing and adorning him.
The housewife moved off a little
   and inspected him,
      inclining her lovely neck to one side.
Noticing the glum look on the poet's face,
   she fell into a joking, mocking mood.
Touching his chin, she said with a laugh,
    'what a pity ! What excellence !
      Oh how nice you look dressed up !'
She brought a mirror;
   Holding it in front of him,
      she said in a voice softened with nectar.
'You'll come back today
   after captivating the hearts
     of the city women
        in your pride then please
don't forget this humble maid servant.
Remember these good services of mine,
   Then you'll have to deck me out
      in fine clothes and ornaments.'
She sat on his lap and held him tight,
   Laughing and setting her cheek against his,
     she began whispering into his ear.
He enjoyed this hugely
   and his lips were soon filled with laughter,
His enchanted heart burst forth,
   overwhelmed with affection,
With deep emotion he said,
    'I won't bother about anything:
      I'll recite such lovely verses
        that I'll be able to bring back
          all the royal treasury
            to your red soled feet.'
His chest puffed up
   while he was saying this.
Holding high his turbaned head,

he opened the door and went swiftly
   to the king's palace.
The poet's wife was overflowing with curiosity;
   She rushed to the window,
      and, smiling inwardly, she peeped out.
Lights began to dance in her black eyes;
   She said to herself, thrilling with delight,
      'So many people are passing by
         on this road;
            I haven't seen a man like mine !'

In the meantime
   the poet's enthusiasm began to abate
      moment by moment.
When he entered the king's palace,
   he was strongly seized with shame;
He felt that he would be relieved
   if only he could die.
These courtiers at the royal place,
   these armed men and guards
      were not at all like his wife !
The rows of beards confused him;
   Had it been wise to come here !
The royal court was not a place
   where one could say a few words
      with affection, with a smile.
Here all were grim-faced,
   from the ministers to the door-keepers.
Why was each man taking on the shape of death
   in the eyes of his fellowmen ?
Pondering this, the poet got no enjoyment,
   His heart was depressed.
Emperor Mahendra Roy was sitting
   as if on the topmost mountain peak,
      coldly, impassively viewing
         the forest of people,
      as if he were a picture
         unshaken, unperturbed.

Streams of kindness and graciousness
   were entertaining the representatives
      of innumerable countries,
The poet filled his sight
   with all this great majesty and glory.
When the deliberations were over,
   there came up, at a sign from a councillor,
      the principal secret spy of the country,
         with folded hands in front of him.
He had the look of a saint,
   There wasn't a sign of corruption on his face,
No one knew that his only business
   was to hunt down men.
He made and kept all kinds of vows,
   Going from home to home he gave pious advice
      to anybody, everybody
         without taking the least fee.
His furtive sideglances dazzled the eyes—
   What had happened and to whom ?
      What were the people doing here and there ?
      He knew the ins and outs of everything.
When he came up, like a Vaishnava,
   wearing a piece of scarf
      printed with the names of deities,
         a councillor said something very secretly
            to the king.
At once the king gave the order:
   'Give him five thousand taka !'
All the courtiers at the court praised the king
   and said, 'Excellent ! Excellent !'
Everyone expressed delight—
   'This award has been given to the most deserving
                                                  one,
      Not a man, woman or child will begrudge this.'
That pious man humbly bowed his head;
   Observing this, one and all expressed approval.
      A wisp of a smile showed on the minister's lips.

Then came a grammarian, shuffling slowly,
  his dusty feet marking up the king's carpet.
On his forehead were beads of perspiration,
  His skin was wrinkled and loose,
    His severe appearance had a look of fury,
      His students dropped dead in terror.
Without looking around, he read out his verses,
  widely opening his mouth in distorted fashion.
It seemed as though he was chewing peas
  mixed with coarse sand.
From beginning to end
  no one understood a thing he said;
    Everyone was sitting with heads bent forward;
      The king said, 'Give him a gift
        with the right hand.'
Then came the astrologer
  whose predictions amazed the king;
    He went away, clinking his coins.
Then came an old man, important and respectable,
  with grass and paddy in his cupped hands.
The king was very generous;
  He filled his bag.
There followed the professional dancers,
  professional singers and the king's priests.
Some came alone,
  Some came with their followers.
Some wore crimson turbans on their heads.
  Some wore yellow ones.
Then came the brahmins, highly respected;
  Some people came for their daughters' needs,
    some for their fathers' obsequies.
Each one got what he deserved,
  Each one got according to his estimate.
That day the king was boundless in his charity,
  They all went off to their respective abodes.
The poet wondered what he should do,
  The king saw him in a corner of the court,
    the picture of embarrassment.

The king said, 'Who's sitting there ?
   Come, councillor; let's find out.'
Rising, the poet said,
   'I'm nobody. I'm only a poet.'
The king said, 'Is that so ! Than come, come.
   We'll talk about your poetry.'
Holding both the poet's hands,
   with great honour the king seated him
      at his side.
The councillor thought to himself,
   'I had better go.
      Now the child's play will begin.'
'Oh emperor,' he said,
   'I have a lot of work;
      I'll go if you give me leave'
The king only waved his hand slightly;
   A king's signal is disinterested;
      Out went all the members of the court—
the councillors, the well-wishers, the ministers,
   the high in rank, the rich, the applicants,
      the complainants, the defendants,
the high, the low, those with different titles—
   like flood waters.

When all the refined and the pious had gone,
   they sat face to face;
The king said. 'Oh poet,
   now start reciting your indescribable poetry.'
Then the poet, holding his cupped hands
      in front of his chest and bowing his head,
   worshipped Saraswati, the goddess of speech—
'Oh Mother, come before me with your smiling face,
   Set the image of your gracious face
      before my sight.
Oh dweller of the pure Lake of Manashi,
   O brightly smiling, O bright robed,
      O honey-tongued, excelling even the
                        sound of the beena,

and sitting on a cluster of lotuses,
I have placed you in my heart;
  I'm always happy in a corner of my room,
    indifferent to worldly interests and abstracted,
      without wealth or honour,
        like a mad person.
Everyone around me is busy in counting
  and taking his or her share
    as they divide the world—
I got heavenly nectar
  when I heard your loving voice;
That's good enough for me,
  still, now and then life cries out.
O Mother of Speech, you know
  man can't relieve his hunger
    with the food of music.
O dearest Mother, what's to be will be,
  I don't worry about that
Just play your beena and start the song,
  that stream from the fountain of nectar
    that will flood the universe—
Hearing this song day and night,
    God enjoys it enormously
      as He moves over this soiled earth,
the song which always vibrates
    like the flame of the sacrificial fire
      which falls over the endless sky
        from the strings of the universal beena,
the song which for ever sounds
    in the cavity of the heart
      and fills life with tears and joy.
Who is where ? Who is coming ? Who is going ?
  Man appears for a moment, vanishes in a moment
    like the play of light-and shade
      on the sands of time !
Today where are all the kings and emperors
  who were here in the past—

Pain, sorrow and shame bloom in the morning
    and fall off in the evening.
There is only among these a tune playing,
    very deep, important, profound, delightful.
It is this
    that fills for ever the engrossed firmament;
Whoever hears that eternal sound
    has set adrift his heart-craft;
He doesn't know himself,
    He doesn't know the world
        or the world's din and bustle.
That person is mad,
    His heart is confused by worry:
        How has he reached your feet
            from the shore of the world
                after tearing off the chains
                    and leaving everything ?
The pure fragrance of your lotus
    is pouring immense delight into my heart
        which hears unheard-of songs
            and unearthly rhythms that are ever new.
Oh Mother, let that beena play !
    Let the world be won over by you !
For a while make it forget
    who is high, who is low,
        who is poor, who is rich,
            who is ahead, who is behind,
                who has won, who has lost,
                    who is good, who is not good,
                        who is superior, who is inferior.
Let there be strung into one song
    all the lowly, all the great
        of this small world—
May it remain happily
    at your feet as a garland.
Oh Saraswati, come with your beena into my heart,
    Reveal your delightful appearance,
        Show me your smile as white as jasmine.

All the planets, the sun, the moon, the stars,
   the whole stream of mankind,
      all the wayfarers from time immemorial
         will drift along in the stream of your song.
I'll be able to see
    the terribly destructive manifestation of Shiva
       clapping his hands
         to the musical time of the rhythm;
The female deities presiding over the ten
   directions have removed their hair-nets
     and are dancing in ten directions.
After saying this much and then pausing,
   the poet, in a doleful voice,
      presented the picture of the sacred story,
        the history of Ram, a descendent of
          King Raghu and the sun of his dynasty—
how he constantly bore unbearable afflictions
   till the last day of his life,
     how he had to pass his days sunk in despair,
     how his life ended in great distress.
He said, 'Recall for a while that day
   when he went to the forest,
      wearing a dirty robe of bark—
with Laksan, his tender-aged brother,
   and Sita the newly married wife,
      without ornaments, languishing in dejection
        like a dark shadow as she got into
         the chariot-of separation.
Loud lamentation sounded in the palace,
    All the citizens were crying on the roads;
       Did such a bolt of lightning ever fall
        on such a place !
His enthronement was to take place,
    Everyone in all directions was rejoicing
       because of that celebration—
The auspicious lamp went out in a moment's storm
    leaving all in darkness.

Think back on that other day
    when venerable Ram with Laksman returned
        to their solitary hut and didn't find
        Janaki (sita), the daughter of King Janaka.
He began to search through the groves,
    calling her repeatedly by her name Janaki
        in grief-stricken wailing.
The large and dense forest with its dark face
    remained silent.
Then think about how it ended,
    Think about the happenings of that day.
That same venerable Sita
    who was to be gained
        after so much grief, so long a separation,
            who was the valued object
                of such austere endeavour,
came into the royal court, submitting to separation
    and bowing down in respect before King Raghu,
and then she disappeared,
    through wounded pride and shame,
        from the divided face of the earth.
Even all such days pass away—
    Where is that unbearable grief
        or even a sign of it—
They have not scorched any endless lines
    on the face of the earth.
The divided surface of the earth
    has been joined together again.
Heaps of flowers are blooming again
    in the Dandak forest.
The wild grass is swaying again
    on the bank of the river Sarju,
        a delightful drawing in green.
Only one tune from that day wails on for ever,
    afflicting the heart in a pleasing
        but doleful melody.

That sublime tune
    which played in that noble heart
       still rings in mankind's ear
          in a magnificent song.
While this was going on,
    very soon all the blood of the Kshatriya caste
                         arrived.
They filled the terror-stricken earth
    with songs of the flood of universal cataclysm,
In an instant all the shores
    were plunged into water.
Who was friend and who was foe was forgotten,
    Streams of blood flowed swiftly,
       The bonds of home were uprooted.
The ocean of death was stirred up into foam,
    The universe watched breathlessly.
The sky trembled as hundreds of eyes closed
    and extinguished the sun and the stars.
When the flood of battle receded,
    Golden Bharat was reduced
       to a deserted and cheerless place,
All the palaces fell to the ground,
    each lying in its own place—
Monstrous peace, sitting on a bloody, muddy bed,
    glared down angrily, speechlessly
       on the face of the earth.
The completion of the Vedic oblation
    was the religious sacrifice of mankind
       in the fire of malice.
The five brothers got the empty golden throne
    after satisfying all their desires
       and destroying all their pride.
The silent palace was melancholy-black;
    The heart-rending lamentations
       of all the helpless palace housewives
          were coming from the burning ground.
All the door-keepers stood in rows
    and welcomed the sons of Pandu
       as victorious heroes.

Today all this may strike us
    as ridiculous and false.
The Bharat that yesterday played Holi
    with the blood of kings,
  filling the sky with the uproar of self-interest
    while forgetting the honour and dignity
                  of the family,
  the next day sat alone with a grieving heart
    in the empty cremation-ground,
      smearing the ashes of the funeral pyre
        and covering her body
           with the garb of an ascetic mendicant.
All the Kurus, all the Pandabs have vanished now,
    All the dreadful sport of fighting is silent.
There are not even any ashes
    from that dreadful funeral pyre.
No one even knows where that land is
    that was the scene of such carnage.
Where was the king ? Where was the capital ?
    Today there is no sign of them.
Then, where is that tune coming from—
    as if that immortal ocean of war
      has taken on new life in one splendid song.
After victory, that voluntary death,
  the great melancholy of those fruitful hopes,
    are offering unworldly peace
      to the heart of everlasting mankind.

'Alas ! On this earth O how many endless
  winters and springs of so many years
    have drifted away smilingly,
      filling the horizon with joy and sadness.
In this way O so many rainy days,
  just like today, have passed away.
    The sky has shed tears with fresh clouds,
    For ages men have gone and men have come.

The distressed have wept,
   The satisfied have laughed,
Lovers have loved just as we ourselves do today.
   They have gone.
      but they have strewn their songs with both hands.
O how many of those songs
   have drifted to land after land,
I look at the earth, green and extensive,
   with enchanted eyes.
I don't know why tears come
   and fill my whole heart.
The beautiful earth is covered
   with the love of O son many people
      and painted with the joys and scrrows
         of O so many days
            and bedaubed with O so many songs
               of endless ages !
I don't want to raise an uproar on this earth
   by arguing,
During the remaining days of my life
   I'll try to satisfy the desires of my heart interiorly.
Let everyone keep whatever he has,
   I don't want to infringe on anyone else's rights,
      Just let me stay peacefully
         in a solitary corner of this earth.
Just give me a flute,
   Let me play it
      to say what's in my mind and heart.
Let me make flowers of song blossom out
   on the forehead of the sky.
Let me create a world of delight,
   gleaning words from my inmost heart.
Let me sprinkle streams of song-nectar
   on the dust of the world.
The spring of the universe
   is constantly cascading
      in tumbling, thundering songs

from the high inaccessible mountain cave
on the peak of creation.
All the planets and stars, all the waves of music
are racing aimlessly through the sky;
I'll take from there
streams of song for this little flute;
I'll fill the green, cupped hands of the earth
with those songs.
With the breeze I'll blend
a pleasant but meaningful message.
Creating new illusions in a fresh monsoon,
I'll paint the deepest shadows;
I'll make it like springtide
and clothe it with the garb of spring.
With fresh lustre I'll make a bit more colourful
the surface of the earth,
the firmament of the sky,
the water of the sea,
the shade of the forest.
I'll leave behind in this earthly life
one or two tunes to make life melodious.
I'll remove some thorns, some obstacles—
then I'll take my leave.
Delighted laughter will be gayer,
Tears will be more beautiful.
The floor of the dwellings,
bedaubed with the nectar of love,
will be more homely.
I will fill the eyes and lips of the sweetheart
with more nectar.
There will be more love, like dew,
on the face of the child.
Man cannot make himself understood,
nor can he himself understand;
Man is wandering about in search of words,
He begs for tunes in a loud, high-pitched voice
like the cooing of the cuckoo.

I'll remove some of that extreme anxiety,
   I'll relieve some of the pain
      stemming from a lack of expression,
         I'll leave behind some melodious words
            before my departure.
Oh Mother Bharati, stay on the seat of my heart,
   At your feet lies my love-lamp.
I don't want to look to anyone else,
   nor do I rely on anyone else.
O how much happiness there was!
   Now all has turned into pain—
O how many friends have turned away!
   O how much eager and expectant love
      has shrivelled up!
Only your feet are beautiful in my heart,
   only that beena plays on and on.
      It affectionately calls out in my heart, saying,
"Come! Leave all of your joys and sorrows.
   Come! Tear off all false bonds.
      Here there is shade
         with everlasting delight,
            with everlasting spring breezes."
Oh Mother, that's good enough;
   Let those go who want to go.
I welcome and choose you once for all;
   I bow down at your lotus-scented feet.

So saying, the poet ended his song;
   He sat down, his eyes enchanted.
His heart began to ring
   like the jingling of a beena.
Thrilling with joy
   and his eyes brimming with tears,
      the king got down from his seat.
His heart overflowing,
   he spread out his arms and embraced the poet.
He said, 'Thank you, poet: thank you.
   My heart is thoroughly overcome with joy.

What more can I say to you ?
  May you live happily for ever !
I can't decide what to give you,
   With what gift can I satisfy you completely ?
     I can give you all the wealth in my treasury.'
Bursting with love
  and eyes brimming with tears, the poet said,
'Take the garland of flowers from your neck
  and put it on my neck.'

After tying the garland to his hair,
  the poet went out on the path—
People were going in various directions,
  on various missions, looking for work.
Some went in palanquins,
  Some raced in chariots.
The poet was returning home,
  self-important, self-satisfied, preoccupied,
    as if his eyes were bewitched,
      as if mentally he was drawing nectar-milk
        from the mythical cow.
The poet's wife was sitting beside the window,
  dressing her hair for the evening
    and wearing a sari as crimson as the twilight.
A delighted smile lit up her face,
  A flock of pigeons surrounded her,
    dancing and calling as they rambled.
She put grains of barley into their beaks leisurely,
  Her mind was thinking
    as fast as her fingers were moving.
Meanwhile, looking toward the path,
  she spotted the poet.
As she waved her arms
  her bracelet bells jingled with sweet music.
She embraced the poet, surrounding him
  with laughter and incomparably happy smiles.
The poet felt jubilant,

Quickly he came up to her and said jokingly,
    yet smiling tenderly,
'Young lady, see what I've brought !
    Various people got various gems.
With great care I brought back
    the garland from the king's neck;
      It is fit to put it round your neck.'
After saying this,
    he unfastened the garland from his hair
      and sought to put it on his beloved's neck.
After saying this,
    he unfastened the garland from his hair
      and sought to put it on his beloved's neck.
His wife angrily pushed his hands away
    and turned aside her face.
In vain she pretended to be angry;
    She felt deep affection in her heart,
      Her fondness filled up with pride,
        In her heart pleasure welled up.
The poet thought:
    'My fate looks gloomy.
      Today I see danger ahead.'
He sat dejected
    with a blank look on his face.
His wife bent over slightly and, from time to time,
    sent sidelong glances his way.
Seeing his mood,
    she laughed out loud
  and removed the edge of her sari from her face.
    The bit of play-acting was over.
In an instant she moved over to his side
    and threw herself on his chest
      and buried her face there,
        alternately laughing and weeping.
Her arms she wrapped round his neck
    and satisfied herself by kissing him
      on the face hundreds of times.

The astounded poet,
    almost beside himself with joy,
        was lost for words.
His devoted wife took the garland
    and lovingly put it on her own neck.
In an outburst of passionate devotion
    the poet thought, as he gazed at that loving face,
        'Lakshmi, the goddess of wealth,
            and Saraswati, the goddess of speech
                are united in a single garland bond.'

MOTHER EARTH

Oh Mother Earth, take me back !
    Take your child to your lap
        under your vast anchal.
Oh Mother Earth, I spread myself over your soil,
    extending myself far and wide
        like the joy of spring.
I drift off into the whole universe,
    from one direction to another,
        toward north, south, east and west,
    cleaving the rib-cage of your bosom,
        breaking the stony bondage of the narrow walls
            of my own dark and cheerless prison,
    swinging and rustling, quivering and falling,
        radiating and dispersing,
            thrilling and startling
                with delight, with light—
I become succulent in the mosses,
    in the tender grass, in the tall grass,
        in branches, in barks, in leaves
            with the secret nectar of life.
With a touch of my fingers
    I set rippling the surface of the grain field,
        bent over with golden heads.

Secretly I fill the fresh petals
   with golden writing, with the scent of nectar,
      with drops of honey.
I dance on the shores of the silent earth
   to the tune of the billowing waves
      as I fill the water of the ocean
         with a blue tinge.
I spread language through the waves
   as I romp jubilantly far and wide.
Like a white stole
   I spread out myself on the mountain peak
      in the spotless snow's lofty seclusion,
         in silent solitude.

The desire that has for a long time
   been arising like a spring in my heart
      without my knowledge,
         gradually filling my whole heart,
            wants to come out to sprinkle you
               in overwhelming streams,
                  violent, free and open.
How can I pierce my heart
   and release from bondage that pained desire
      and send it far and wide, from land to land
         in immense streams !
Just sitting in a corner of my room
   with my avid heart I am absorbed in reading
                                    constantly
      to see who is travelling far and wide
         to other places out of curiosity;
With them I enclose you in my heart
   through the enchantment of illusion.

A far-off country, very difficult of access,
   an endless wasteland desolate and trackless,
a battlefield of immense thirst,
   blazing sands that pierce the eyes with needles—

it seems as if the fever-stricken earth
  is wallowing on a bed of sand
    that stretches to the horizon,
  inflamed in body, hot of breath,
    parched-voiced, bereft of companions,
      silent, severe.
Oh for how many days,
  sitting beside the window at the end of the house,
    staring in front of me,
    I have mentally drawn distant scenes;
All around there are mountain ranges,
  There is a blue lake, soundless and solitary
    and crystal-clear,
Scattered clouds are lying down,
  hugging the peaks like suckling babes,
Far away snow-crested blue mountain ranges
  bar the view;
It seems as though,
  row on row, these sky-piercing ranges
    rise like a fixed interdiction
      at the door of Shiva's hermitage
        where He is in yogic contemplation.
In my fancying I travel to a far-off seashore
  in the great polar region—
where the earth has taken a vow
  of perpetual maidenhood, robed in snow,
    solitary, detached, unadorned;
where, at the end of the long night,
  day comes back, soundless, songless;
where night comes,
  but there is no one to go to sleep;
in the endless sky
  night, staring ahead and sleepless,
    stays awake by the empty bed
      like the mother of a dead child.
The more I read the names of new countries,
  the more I hear picturesque accounts,

the more my heart goes out
and wants to touch everything—
a cluster of homes on the lake shore
among the gorges of the small blue mountains,
nets drying on the shore,
boats drifting on the water,
their sails unfurled
as fishermen try to catch fish,
a narrow stream zigzagging somehow
down the mountain pass;
I wish to embrace that lonesome home
near the thundering rapids,
cosily sitting on the solitary lap
of the mountain.
I wish to take as my own
whatever there is, wherever it is;
I wish to dissolve myself
in the water of the river and distribute water
to quench the thirst in new homes
on both shores
singing sweet and low songs day and night
as I go.
The highest mountain is beautiful
in its own incomprehensible mystery,
spreading itself out
in the middle of the earth
from the rising lake
to the setting sea,
secretly spawning and hiding new races
in the lap of the hard stones,
in the harsh cold winds.
In my imagination I want to be of the same race
with all the people of the world
in countries far and near;
I wish to drink camel's milk and grow up
in the desert as an Arabian child,
unruly, unrestrained;

I wish to travel to an aloof, stony city
   to a Buddhist monastery
     in the mountain region of Tibet.
I wish to be born in the homes of all—
   a Persian, drinking grape juice
     and living in a rose garden,
   a fearless Tartar mounted on his horse,
   a courteous, energetic Japanese,
   a wise and ancient Chinese,
     busy day and night.
I like barbarism;
   healthy, strong, fierce and naked;
there is no right or wrong, no customs,
   no prohibition or restraint, no anxious care,
     no question of one's own or another's—
where the unbounded streams of life
   are flowing day and night,
     striking out ahead, sustaining blows unperturbedly,
where life does not look at the past
   stricken with regret
nor to the future
   with unrealizable longing,
that life goes on dancing intensely, delightedly
   on the crests of the waves of the present;
I love too the life that is not orderly,
   that is even wayward;
Oh how I yearn to race full sail
   like a light craft !
The ferocious forest tiger carries his huge frame
   effortlessly, by his own furious might;
His body is blazing bright
   like the hidden fire in lightning
     in the forest clouds.
With a frightening growl deep as thunder
   he falls on his unwary prey
     with the speed of lightning.

I desire to enjoy that easy grace,
   that maliciously intense pleasure,
     that haughty pride;
Over and over I wish to satisfy my thirst
   by drinking from all the vessels of the universe
     the ever-new streams
       of that rich, that heady wine.

Oh Beautiful ! Oh Earth !
   while gazing at you oh how many times
   my heart began to sing in stupendous delight.
I wished to grasp you about your waist
   girdled with oceans,
day and night, endlessly and in all directions
   to dance like the morning light
     on the waves of the quivering leaves
       in the forests, on the hills,
   diffusing myself everywhere
     like the rays of the dawn sun,
   kissing each and every flower bud,
     embracing the soft and green meadows,
   swinging all day long in a cradle of delight
     on each and every wave.
I wished to go silently on tiptoe
   like universal sleep, brushing my hand lightly
     over the eyes of all your beasts and birds,
Going from bed to bed, from abode to abode,
   from home to home, from cave to cave
     I would cover you with cool darkness
       as with a vast anchal.
Oh Earth, you have been mine for many years,
   Mingling me with your clay,
     you go through the endless sky round the sun
       with untiring steps.
For endless days and nights, for ages and ages
   your grasses have grown,
     your flowers have blossomed profusely,·

your trees have showered leaves, flowers,
    fruits and pollen fragrance into my heart.
So now, from time to time
  as I sit alone and absent-minded
    on the bank of the Padma,
      I open my bewitched eyes
        and with my whole body, with my whole
                                            heart
I feel—
  how the tips of the grasses thrill
    on your soil,
  how the stream of life sap is circulating
    day and night in your heart,
  how, overflowing with blind joy,
    the flower buds bloom
      on the lovely tips of the stalks,
  how, in the fresh sunlight, trees and creepers,
    the grasses and bushes thrill with secret delight
      in obsessed pleasure like a babe
        tired but satisfied after suckling,
          dreaming happily, its face smiling.
So now, on occasion, extreme agitation
  awakes within me
    when the sun-rays of autumn fall on the
                                        golden field
      full of ripe heads,
    when the wind-blown coconut trees
      quiver in the wind, sparkling in the light—
I'm thinking of the day
  when my heart was all-pervading
    on land and water, in the abode of the forest
                                              leaves,
      in the blue tinge of the sky.
It seems as if the universe is calling me constantly
  in an indistinct voice.
It seems I can hear,
  from that wonderful and vast playground,

      like the confused rustling of leaves,
    the never-ending sound
        of my friends' various and familiar voices
          at joyful play.
Oh take me back there just once.
    Banish that feeling of separation
      which occasionally comes into my heart
    when I see ahead of me, in the twilight's rays,
      a vast tract of grass-land,
    when cows, kicking up dust, return
      by a path in a field from a distant pasture,
    when a smoke-line rises
      from a tree bound hamlet,
    when, in the distance,
      the moon slowly shows herself
        like a weary wayfarer
          on a lonely, sandy river bank;
I think of myself as lonely as one living abroad,
    I want to run about, spreading out my arms
      and take the whole outside into my heart—
        this sky, this earth,
          the bright, tranquil, sleeping moonlight
          on this river !
I am not able to touch anything;
    I only stare blankly, sunk in depression.
Take me back into that wholeness from where
    life is constantly sprouting, budding, blooming
      in numberless forms,
    songs are resounding in innumerable tunes,
      dances are welling up in countless
        gestures and movements,
    the heart is drifting on streams of emotion,
      the flute is playing through every opening.
Oh celestial green wishing-cow,
    you are standing still;
The uncountable thirsty life forms,
    the creepers and trees, the beasts and birds,
      are all milking you from all directions;

The nectar of joy is pouring down
  in oh so many ways and forms,
    The ten directions resound
      with songs of intense delight.
Oned with everything, in an instant
  I will experience all that wonderful joy
    of the universe,
Will not your forests be greener with my joy ?
  In the dawn light
    won't new glittering rays be diffused ?
The surface of the sky, of the earth
  will be coloured with the enchanted emotions
    of my heart—
When a poet sees something,
  in his heart, it will become a poem,
The eyes of a lover
  will see with obsessive emotion,
    The birds will sing unexpectedly.
Oh Earth ! The whole of your body
  has become colourful with the pleasure of all.
How often the streams of life have come,
  have gone away, embellishing you
    with their own lives,
They mingled the love of their hearts
  with your clay.
They wrote so many things,
  strewing the embraces of their anxious hearts
    in all directions:
With all this I will carefully mingle all my love
  and colour your anchal with living colours,
    I'll decorate you with all that I have.
From the river bank won't some enchanted ear
  hear my song in the river water ?
Won't some dwellers of the earth,
  awaking from sleep,
    see my smile in the splendour of the dawn ?
Today, at the end of the century

won't my heart beat
   in the heaps of beautiful forest leaves ?
Oh how many men and women will live
   their domestic lives in home after home;
      won't I stay on a bit in their affection ?
Won't I come down like a smile on their faces,
   like charming youth into their whole bodies,
like unexpected happiness in their spring days,
   like a sprout of love, eagerly expectant,
      into their hearts ?
Oh Motherland, will you abandon me completely ?
   Will the firm earthen bonds of age after age
      be torn all at once ?
Will I have to go,
   leaving behind the comforting lap
      of endless ages ?
All these trees and creepers,
   these hills, rivers and forests,
this eternally blue sky,
   the open breeze, full of life,
      the wakeful light,
the society-of-life,
   stringing into a garland the hearts
      of all creatures—
         won't they pull me from all directions ?
I would surround you in my wanderings,
   I would remain among your dear ones;
You will call me repeatedly
   and take me into your heart, warm with life
just as you call the insects, beasts and birds,
   the creepers and shrubs;
In age after age, in life after life
   you will suckle me
      with endless and profound affection,
      feeding me the sweet nectar of your breast milk
         in the form of immense delight,
   and so you will satisfy

      the great and innumerable needs
         of life's craving.
After that, I, a young son of the earth,
   will go out among the continents of the world
      to the distant celestial sphere
         by a well-nigh inaccessible path.
All my desires have not yet been fulfilled,
   There is still the thirst
      for the nectar of your affection.
Your face still awakes happy dreams
   in my eyes,
I have not at all finished with the the whole of you,
   Everything is full of mystery to me.
My steadfast gaze
   finds no end to your wonders.
Like a babe
   I am still on your bosom,
      looking at your face.
Oh Mother, grasp me with the strong bonds
   of your embrace.
Take me into that secret abode
   from where your vast life rises up
      as the spring of wonderful bliss—
         Don't keep me at a distance.

ILLUSIONISM

Ah ! cheerless land,
   wearing your emaciated old age,
      bearing the burden of erudition,
you have come to learn,
   with your clever and fine insight,
      that God's deception now lies exposed !

Sitting idly day and night
   in a corner of your room

with your keen intellect
    honed razor-sharp,
you have assumed
    that the whole universe is a myth—
        creation, full of stars and planets
            in the boundless sky.

For ages and ages
    all the beasts, birds and other creatures,
        have been breathing here firm and fearless,
    taking God's world as their mother's lap;
You shaggy, hoary one,
    you don't believe anything !
The fair of this world
    consists of countless creatures;
        you think this is all childish imagining !

A GAME

Let it be a game,
    I have to join in with the world
        that is overflowing with roaring waves
            of delight.
Where will you keep sitting
    in some dark corner of your heart
        after giving up everything !
You should know
    that you are nothing but a child
        in this vast world,
            in the lap of endless ages,
                in the courtyard of the sky—
The more you know
    the more you should think
        that you know nothing.
Take with submission, faith and love
    the great toy, that plaything

full of colours, fragrance and songs
  which your mother has given you.
Even if it is but dust, let it be but dust;
  This dust is incomparable !
Don't stay that way, sitting all alone,
  grown old before your time.
    How can you grow up
      if you don't want to play.

BOND

A bond ? Of course it's a bond.
  Everything is a bond—
    affection, love, the longing for happiness;
That's nothing but the hand of your mother
  taking you from one breast to the other,
    letting you drink fresh streams of delight
      to your heart's content.
A baby has a thirst for breast milk
  as for something good for it—
In the same way
  there is a natural thirst
    that attracts the hope, love and delight
      of the world
        in oh so much happiness,
          in oh so much pain;
That inborn longing is shaping, birth after birth,
  the life that is difficult to attain,
    the one that fills our lives and hearts;
At every moment new desires and hopes
  are taking you to new experiences,
    new hermitages.
By some mistaken notions of freedom
  you want to tear off the bonds
    attaching you to your mother
      and so destroy your thirst for breast milk.

MOTION

I know
  that life is full of joys and sorrows,
    smiles and tears,
  that cruel bonds form knots and knots of scars.
I know
  that in the churning of the ocean
    of earthly life,
      it is someone's luck to get nectar,
        someone's luck to get deadly poison.
I don't know
  why all this happens
    or how this system will work out in the end.
I don't know what will happen in future,
  All is darkness in this world
    from beginning to end—
I don't know
  whether or not there is an end to all griefs,
    whether the craving for happiness
      can satisfy eternal hopes.
I don't want to know about the mystery of life
  at the doors of the pundits.
I don't want to tear by myself
  the world-wide bonds—
I have only one way to go—
  it's with the countless creatures
    of this world.

SALVATION

If I'm only concerned about my own little soul
  and if I close everything—
    my eyes and ears, my intelligence and mind—
  and if I turn away from the whole world,
    no one knows where I have to go
      in hope of salvation !

At my side the great ship of the universe
  will sail by,
    overwhelming the firmament
      with the songs of the pilgrims,
      filling all sides with a bright sail of sunbeams,
        with countless hearts
          full of wondrous beauty.
Gradually all the smiles and tears,
  all the light and darkness
    will fade away in the distance,
  all the sadness and grief
    that fill the endless world
      will drift away in a doleful tune
        into the great void.
If the whole world goes away weeping,
  will I stay behind in the tomb of salvation ?

POWERLESS

I belong to the place
  to which I have come,
    I am a needy child in a needy world.
I accept the whole burden of happiness and misery
  as my good fortune obtained since my birth;
    This I have resolved.
Oh Earthen Mother, green and all-patient,
  you don't have unlimited wealth !
You want to provide food for all,
  but often you are unable to do so—
With pale faces and parched mouths
  your sons and daughters lament, saying,
    'Where oh where is food ?'
Oh Mother, I know
  that in your hands there is only imperfect
                      happiness—
Whatever you form
  constantly breaks into pieces;

Death, the omnivorous one,
  puts his hand into everything;
Alas ! You can't fulfil all our hopes—
  Ought I leave your warm heart on that account !

POOR ONE

Oh Earth, I love you the more
  simply because you are indigent, deficient;
    I enjoy your affection even more—
My inmost heart is afflicted
  when I see the doleful smile
    on your pain-stricken face.
With the love-blood of your heart
  you have given life to your child,
You are gazing at him day and night,
  Even with all your affection
    you can't give him nectar.
Oh for how many ages
  you have been creating a joy-home
    with colours, fragrances and songs,
Even today it's not over
  during the day, during the night.
It's not heaven,
  You have created the shadow of heaven.
So your face is gentle with sadness,
  All your beauty is drenched with tears.

SELF-DEDICATION

I'll set your joy-song to music
  with a few pleasant strains
    that I have in my heart;
In your sad weeping my voice will ring out,
  becoming melancholy with your voice;

I'll revere you
  with flowers and sandalwood paste,
    applying vermillion to the parting of your hair;
      I'll arrange an attractive hair do;
I'll make you swing
  on the waves of the sea of pleasure,
    with new strains, with new lyrics.
I have no more human pride;
   When I gaze at your soft, green motherly face,
    I love your dust and soil.
I'll not run away in scorn
  to find heaven and salvation
    while ignoring the lap of the earth
      where I was born.

FIRM REMEMBRANCE

Remembrance, firm as a white, motionless mountain,
  is constantly awake and alert
    on the surface of my heart.
Encircling that silent, snowy mountain,
  all my days, all my nights come and go.

In the deepest part of my heart
  she has set her feet—
She raises her lofty head
  above all that is mine.
My hundreds of imaginings,
  like colourful clouds,
    laugh and weep as they surround her,
      hanging low with affection.

My green creeper,
  with its burden of flowers and leaves,
    wants to bind her in a succulent, soft embrace.
Day and night the bird-of-desire flies alone

to the desolate mountain peak
   that disappears in the sky
      and that is nigh-impossible to reach.

All about her there is so much coming and going,
   so many songs, so many words—
In the midst of all this, like meditation,
   there is only motionless silence.
Yet, from afar
   I can see that solitary mountain peak
      all by itself.
The eternal snow-line is limned
   on the heart of the sky.

THORN TREE

Once, in the light of dawn,
   a bird was singing delightedly,
Casting a side-glance,
   the thorn tree said to the flower—
'You are nothing but a delicate, pleasure loving
                                        flower,
   The wind sways you
      and your life comes to an end
         with the passing of the light of day !
On one side are the bees,
   overwhelmed by the intoxication of honey.
On the other side there is the wind,
   the thief of fragrance—
Oh darling of the forest, I feel like laughing
   on seeing the love you get.
Oh how wonderful !
   What a colourful robe you wear !
There is no end to the affection and smiles
   you enjoy.
All day long your are engrossed in
   delight bedaubed with fragrance.

Alas ! How long will you be occupied
  in this game of pleasure—
    charming beauty, gaudy luxury,
      the honey-bee fair.

'Alas ! I am not a pleasure loving creature
  like you—
I don't know anything about gestures and deportment,
  smiles and colourful robes.
I'm uncovered,
  attached to the earth by my own strength—
Who can drive me away ?
  Who can grind me into the ground ?
I am not short-lived like you,
  In this world I stay on for ever,
    I'm not afraid of rain or storm.
I'm always alone, friendless—
  I owe love to no one,
    I don't waste day and night
      listening to flattery.
Winter will come one day,
  The songs of the birds will stop,
All the leaves and flowers will fall off,
  I'll remain as before.

Look at me !
  There's no excess anywhere—
Everything is clear,
  Everyone knows what I'm worth.
One who is tough and harsh
  owns this faint-hearted, cowardly world.
I can leave my own mark
  by scraping with my nails.
Some fan the earth.
  Some lightly brush a soft hand over the feet,
Some bow their heads,
  wallowing on the ground in obeisance—

Many people cajole, entice and deceive others
   through various stratagems—
Some have colours,
   Some have sweet scents,
Useless is bridal chamber attire,
   It's only for a few days.
I don't do anything at all,
   I've only pierced the heart of the earth
      while standing silently, head held high.

You don't even glance at me
   out of the corner of your eye,
Secretly bursting with pride,
   you blossom out.
You have honey, I have none—
   Keep it for yourself.
You have beauty,
   Nobody looks at me.
Some have branches, some have leaves,
   some have flowers, some bear fruit—
      Only my hand is empty day and night.
Oh you trees !
   You are huge and old,
      You are indifferent to us—
I'm not big, I provide no shade.
   I'm insignificant and small.
Though I'm mean and contemptible,
   still I'm destructive and fearful—
My wretchedness is my army
   which will win out.

AIMLESS JOURNEY

Oh Beauty, how much further will you take me ?
   Tell me on what shore your Golden Craft will dock.
Oh Exotic, whenever I ask you,
   you only smile sweetly—

I don't know
   what you have in mind.
You show me the direction by raising your finger
   and pointing to the shoreless ocean
      that is restless, eager, overflowing
         and to the sun setting in the distant west
            in a corner of the sky.
What is there ?
   What am I to search for ?

Oh Unknown, tell me; I'm asking you—
   Is your abode there where day's funeral pyre
      is burning on the shore of the evening ?
where the water is shining like liquid fire ?
   where the surface of the sky is melting ?
where, it seems, the ten direction-maidens
   are shedding copious tears ?
at the foot of the cloud-kissing mountains
   behind which the sun sets
on the shore of the sea
   resounding with crashing waves ?
You only smile and look at me
   without saying anything.

The wind is always howling,
   The high tide is rumbling, going at high speed.
Apprehensive is the deep blue water,
   Nowhere can I see the shore,
It seems as if
   endless lamentations are swaying the world.
On it sails the Golden Craft,
   On it fall the evening rays,
Why, on it, do you
   only sit and smile your sweet smile ?

When you first called me, saying,
   'Who will go with me',
for a while I looked into your eyes

in the fresh dawn
Spreading out your hands in front of you,
   you pointed out to me
     the boundless ocean in the west,
The light, restless as hope,
   was shimmering on the water.
Then, getting into the Craft, I asked you,
   Is there new life there ?
     Do the dreams of hope
       grow into golden fruit there ?
Looking at me without speaking,
   you only smiled.

At times clouds showed up,
   sometimes the sun—
At times the ocean became billowy,
   sometimes it was the picture of peace.
The day is passing,
   The wind is striking the sail,
The Golden Craft is sailing on,
   In the west I saw the sun setting on the mountain.

I'm asking you just one more time,
   'Is calm death there—
     Is peace there ? Is sleep there in the darkness ?'

Spreading her wings, the dark night will come now,
   The golden glow of evening will be veiled.
Only the fragrance of your body will drift about,
   Only the sound of waves will reach my ears.
Locks of your hair will flair out in the air
   and will fall on my body—
My heart will be confused,
   My body will lose control of itself,
Agitated, I'll call out,
   'Oh where are you ? Come here and touch me !'
You won't reply,
   I won't see your silent smile.